Early Medieval Monarc

THE FAMILIAL RELATIONSHIPS THROUGH MARRIAGES

This is part of a series of books on the early history of Europe. This series documents many of the complex relationships of the monarchies of early Europe, including England, Scotland, France, Spain, Hungary, and Germany. These other family histories are necessary to fully understand the political pressures that evolved the monarchies in the various countries.

Original source documentation is embedded. Some of the royal family histories, particularly those of Spain and Hungary, are rare in English.

External links to a website with the histories of the supporting dukes, counts, and knights is provided.

Important Notes

The numbers (**#########**) **or** a royal person's name can be used to search the website "**Many Mini Biographies**" (www.teachergenealogist007.com) for details on the lives of all the royal persons or families. The website has a "**search**" box.

§§ before a name indicates that the person has no additional historical information in this series.

Abbreviations:
"**s/o**" is "son of"; "**d/o**" is "daughter of"

Ancestral Charts for Three Generations

Chart #1

Ancestors of King Edward III Plantagenet

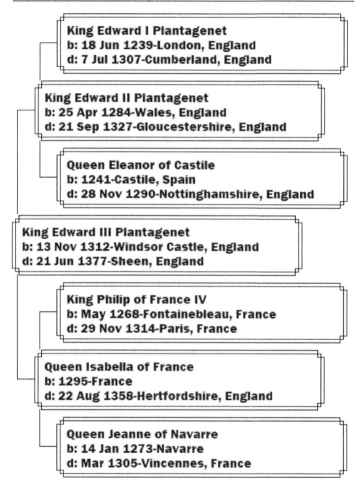

King Edward I Plantagenet
b: 18 Jun 1239-London, England
d: 7 Jul 1307-Cumberland, England

King Edward II Plantagenet
b: 25 Apr 1284-Wales, England
d: 21 Sep 1327-Gloucestershire, England

Queen Eleanor of Castile
b: 1241-Castile, Spain
d: 28 Nov 1290-Nottinghamshire, England

King Edward III Plantagenet
b: 13 Nov 1312-Windsor Castle, England
d: 21 Jun 1377-Sheen, England

King Philip of France IV
b: May 1268-Fontainebleau, France
d: 29 Nov 1314-Paris, France

Queen Isabella of France
b: 1295-France
d: 22 Aug 1358-Hertfordshire, England

Queen Jeanne of Navarre
b: 14 Jan 1273-Navarre
d: Mar 1305-Vincennes, France

Chart #2

Ancestors of King Edward I Plantagenet

King John Plantagenet
b: 26 Dec 1166-Lincolnshire, England
m: 24 Aug 1200-France
d: 18 Oct 1216-Newark, Nottinghamshire

King Henry III Plantagenet
b: 10 Oct 1206-London, England
m: 14 Jan 1236-London, England
d: 16 Nov 1272-London, England

Queen Isabella of Angouleme
b: 1188-France
d: 31 May 1246-France

King Edward I Plantagenet
b: 18 Jun 1239-London, England
d: 7 Jul 1307-Cumberland, England

Count Raymond Berengar
b: 1195-France
m: 15 Jun 1219-France
d: 19 Aug 1245-Provence, France

Queen Eleanor of Provence
b: 1223-France
d: 26 Jun 1291-Wiltshire, England

Countess Beatrice of Savoia
b: by 1207-Savoy
d: 1265-France

Chart #3

Ancestors of Queen Eleanor of Castile

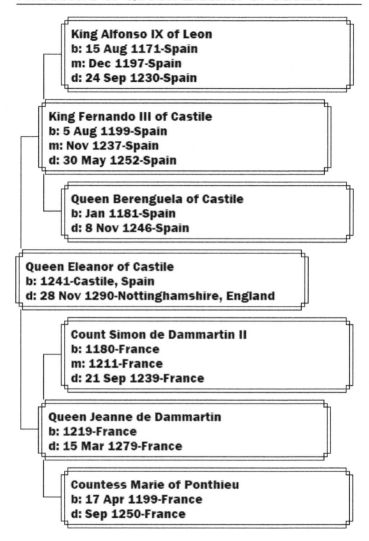

King Alfonso IX of Leon
b: 15 Aug 1171-Spain
m: Dec 1197-Spain
d: 24 Sep 1230-Spain

King Fernando III of Castile
b: 5 Aug 1199-Spain
m: Nov 1237-Spain
d: 30 May 1252-Spain

Queen Berenguela of Castile
b: Jan 1181-Spain
d: 8 Nov 1246-Spain

Queen Eleanor of Castile
b: 1241-Castile, Spain
d: 28 Nov 1290-Nottinghamshire, England

Count Simon de Dammartin II
b: 1180-France
m: 1211-France
d: 21 Sep 1239-France

Queen Jeanne de Dammartin
b: 1219-France
d: 15 Mar 1279-France

Countess Marie of Ponthieu
b: 17 Apr 1199-France
d: Sep 1250-France

Chart #4

Ancestors of King Philip IV of France

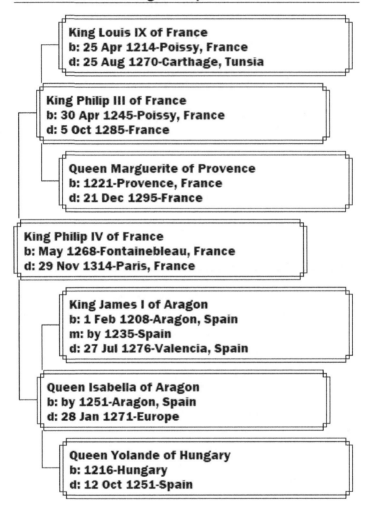

King Louis IX of France
b: 25 Apr 1214-Poissy, France
d: 25 Aug 1270-Carthage, Tunsia

King Philip III of France
b: 30 Apr 1245-Poissy, France
d: 5 Oct 1285-France

Queen Marguerite of Provence
b: 1221-Provence, France
d: 21 Dec 1295-France

King Philip IV of France
b: May 1268-Fontainebleau, France
d: 29 Nov 1314-Paris, France

King James I of Aragon
b: 1 Feb 1208-Aragon, Spain
m: by 1235-Spain
d: 27 Jul 1276-Valencia, Spain

Queen Isabella of Aragon
b: by 1251-Aragon, Spain
d: 28 Jan 1271-Europe

Queen Yolande of Hungary
b: 1216-Hungary
d: 12 Oct 1251-Spain

Chart #5

Ancestors of Queen Jeanne of Navarre

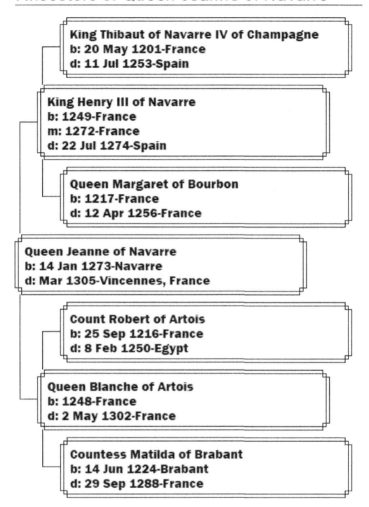

King Thibaut of Navarre IV of Champagne
b: 20 May 1201-France
d: 11 Jul 1253-Spain

King Henry III of Navarre
b: 1249-France
m: 1272-France
d: 22 Jul 1274-Spain

Queen Margaret of Bourbon
b: 1217-France
d: 12 Apr 1256-France

Queen Jeanne of Navarre
b: 14 Jan 1273-Navarre
d: Mar 1305-Vincennes, France

Count Robert of Artois
b: 25 Sep 1216-France
d: 8 Feb 1250-Egypt

Queen Blanche of Artois
b: 1248-France
d: 2 May 1302-France

Countess Matilda of Brabant
b: 14 Jun 1224-Brabant
d: 29 Sep 1288-France

Chart #6

Ancestors of King John Plantagenet

Comte Geoffrey Plantagenet
b: 24 Aug 1113-Anjou, France
d: 7 Sep 1151-Le Mans, Maine, France

King Henry II Plantagenet
b: 5 Mar 1133-Le Mans, Maine, France
m: 18 May 1152-Poitiers, France
d: 6 Jul 1189-France

Empress Matilda fitz Roy
b: Mar 1102-Oxfordshire, England
d: 10 Sep 1167-Rouen, Normandy, France

King John Plantagenet
b: 26 Dec 1166-Lincolnshire, England
d: 18 Oct 1216-Newark, Nottinghamshire

Duke Guillaume of Aquitaine
b: 1099-Toulouse, France
m: 1121-France
d: 19 Apr 1137-Spain

Queen Eleanor of Aquitaine
b: 1122-Aquitaine, France
d: 31 Mar 1204-France

Duchess Aenor of Chatellerault
b: abt 1105-France
d: 1130-France

Chart #7

Ancestors of King Alfonso IX of Leon

Emperor Alfonso VII of Spain
b: 1 Mar 1105-Spain
d: 21 Aug 1157-Spain

King Ferdinand II of Leon
b: 1137-Spain
m: Jun 1165-Portugal
d: 22 Jan 1188-Spain

Empress Berenguela of Barcelona
b: 1116-Barcelona, Spain
d: aft 1149-Spain

King Alfonso IX of Leon
b: 15 Aug 1171-Spain
d: 24 Sep 1230-Spain

King Alfonso of Portugal
b: 1109–12-Portugal
m: 1146-Savoy
d: 8 Dec 1185-Portugal

Queen Urraca of Portugal
b: 1148-Portugal
d: aft 1211-Spain

Queen Mafalda of Savoy
b: 1125-Savoy
d: 1196-Portugal

Chart #8

Ancestors of Queen Berenguela of Castile

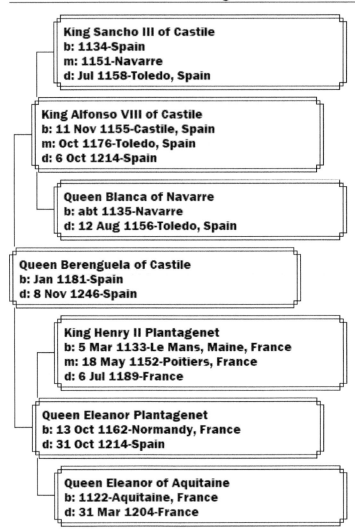

King Sancho III of Castile
b: 1134-Spain
m: 1151-Navarre
d: Jul 1158-Toledo, Spain

King Alfonso VIII of Castile
b: 11 Nov 1155-Castile, Spain
m: Oct 1176-Toledo, Spain
d: 6 Oct 1214-Spain

Queen Blanca of Navarre
b: abt 1135-Navarre
d: 12 Aug 1156-Toledo, Spain

Queen Berenguela of Castile
b: Jan 1181-Spain
d: 8 Nov 1246-Spain

King Henry II Plantagenet
b: 5 Mar 1133-Le Mans, Maine, France
m: 18 May 1152-Poitiers, France
d: 6 Jul 1189-France

Queen Eleanor Plantagenet
b: 13 Oct 1162-Normandy, France
d: 31 Oct 1214-Spain

Queen Eleanor of Aquitaine
b: 1122-Aquitaine, France
d: 31 Mar 1204-France

Chart #9

Ancestors of King Louis IX of France

King Philip II Augustus Capet
b: 21 Aug 1165-France
d: 14 Jul 1223-France

King Louis VIII Capet
b: 5 Sep 1187-Paris, France
d: 8 Nov 1226-France

Queen Isabelle of Hainaut
b: 5 Apr 1170-Hainaut
d: 14 Mar 1190-France

King Louis IX of France
b: 25 Apr 1214-Poissy, France
d: 25 Aug 1270-Carthage, Tunsia

King Alfonso VIII of Castile
b: 11 Nov 1155-Castile, Spain
m: Oct 1176-Toledo, Spain
d: 6 Oct 1214-Spain

Queen Blanche of Castile
b: 4 Mar 1188-Castile, Spain
d: 26 Nov 1252-Paris, France

Queen Eleanor Plantagenet
b: 13 Oct 1162-Normandy, France
d: 31 Oct 1214-Spain

Chart #10
Ancestors of King James I of Aragon

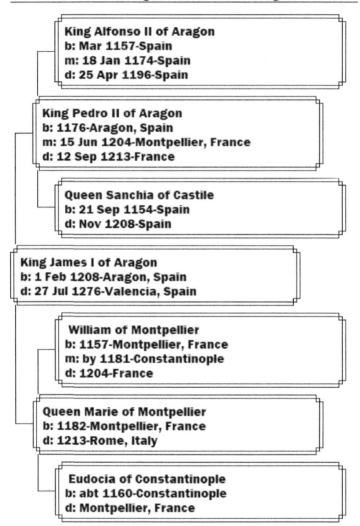

King Alfonso II of Aragon
b: Mar 1157-Spain
m: 18 Jan 1174-Spain
d: 25 Apr 1196-Spain

King Pedro II of Aragon
b: 1176-Aragon, Spain
m: 15 Jun 1204-Montpellier, France
d: 12 Sep 1213-France

Queen Sanchia of Castile
b: 21 Sep 1154-Spain
d: Nov 1208-Spain

King James I of Aragon
b: 1 Feb 1208-Aragon, Spain
d: 27 Jul 1276-Valencia, Spain

William of Montpellier
b: 1157-Montpellier, France
m: by 1181-Constantinople
d: 1204-France

Queen Marie of Montpellier
b: 1182-Montpellier, France
d: 1213-Rome, Italy

Eudocia of Constantinople
b: abt 1160-Constantinople
d: Montpellier, France

Chart #11

Ancestors of Queen Yolande of Hungary

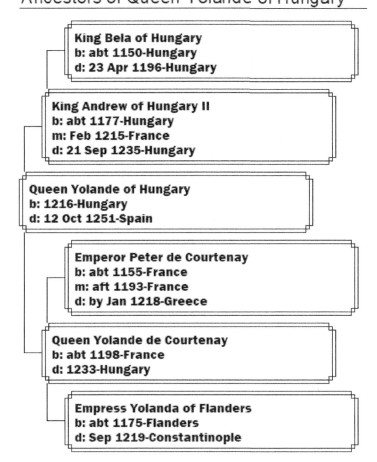

King Bela of Hungary
b: abt 1150-Hungary
d: 23 Apr 1196-Hungary

King Andrew of Hungary II
b: abt 1177-Hungary
m: Feb 1215-France
d: 21 Sep 1235-Hungary

Queen Yolande of Hungary
b: 1216-Hungary
d: 12 Oct 1251-Spain

Emperor Peter de Courtenay
b: abt 1155-France
m: aft 1193-France
d: by Jan 1218-Greece

Queen Yolande de Courtenay
b: abt 1198-France
d: 1233-Hungary

Empress Yolanda of Flanders
b: abt 1175-Flanders
d: Sep 1219-Constantinople

Chart #12

Ancestors of Empress Matilda fitz Roy

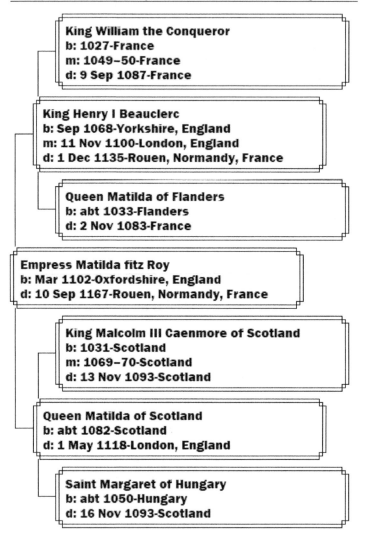

King William the Conqueror
b: 1027-France
m: 1049–50-France
d: 9 Sep 1087-France

King Henry I Beauclerc
b: Sep 1068-Yorkshire, England
m: 11 Nov 1100-London, England
d: 1 Dec 1135-Rouen, Normandy, France

Queen Matilda of Flanders
b: abt 1033-Flanders
d: 2 Nov 1083-France

Empress Matilda fitz Roy
b: Mar 1102-Oxfordshire, England
d: 10 Sep 1167-Rouen, Normandy, France

King Malcolm III Caenmore of Scotland
b: 1031-Scotland
m: 1069–70-Scotland
d: 13 Nov 1093-Scotland

Queen Matilda of Scotland
b: abt 1082-Scotland
d: 1 May 1118-London, England

Saint Margaret of Hungary
b: abt 1050-Hungary
d: 16 Nov 1093-Scotland

Chart #13

Ancestors of Emperor Alfonso VII of Spain

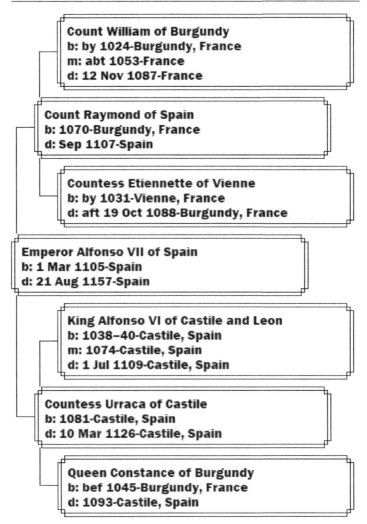

Count William of Burgundy
b: by 1024-Burgundy, France
m: abt 1053-France
d: 12 Nov 1087-France

Count Raymond of Spain
b: 1070-Burgundy, France
d: Sep 1107-Spain

Countess Etiennette of Vienne
b: by 1031-Vienne, France
d: aft 19 Oct 1088-Burgundy, France

Emperor Alfonso VII of Spain
b: 1 Mar 1105-Spain
d: 21 Aug 1157-Spain

King Alfonso VI of Castile and Leon
b: 1038–40-Castile, Spain
m: 1074-Castile, Spain
d: 1 Jul 1109-Castile, Spain

Countess Urraca of Castile
b: 1081-Castile, Spain
d: 10 Mar 1126-Castile, Spain

Queen Constance of Burgundy
b: bef 1045-Burgundy, France
d: 1093-Castile, Spain

Chart #14

Ancestors of King Alfonso of Portugal

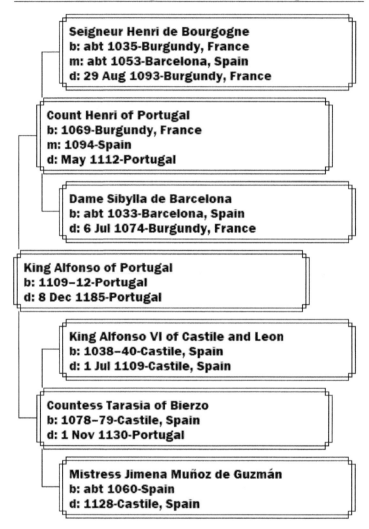

Seigneur Henri de Bourgogne
b: abt 1035-Burgundy, France
m: abt 1053-Barcelona, Spain
d: 29 Aug 1093-Burgundy, France

Count Henri of Portugal
b: 1069-Burgundy, France
m: 1094-Spain
d: May 1112-Portugal

Dame Sibylla de Barcelona
b: abt 1033-Barcelona, Spain
d: 6 Jul 1074-Burgundy, France

King Alfonso of Portugal
b: 1109–12-Portugal
d: 8 Dec 1185-Portugal

King Alfonso VI of Castile and Leon
b: 1038–40-Castile, Spain
d: 1 Jul 1109-Castile, Spain

Countess Tarasia of Bierzo
b: 1078–79-Castile, Spain
d: 1 Nov 1130-Portugal

Mistress Jimena Muñoz de Guzmán
b: abt 1060-Spain
d: 1128-Castile, Spain

Chart #15

Ancestors of King Sancho III of Castile

Count Raymond of Spain
b: 1070-Burgundy, France
d: Sep 1107-Spain

Emperor Alfonso VII of Spain
b: 1 Mar 1105-Spain
d: 21 Aug 1157-Spain

Countess Urraca of Castile
b: 1081-Castile, Spain
d: 10 Mar 1126-Castile, Spain

King Sancho III of Castile
b: 1134-Spain
d: Jul 1158-Toledo, Spain

Ramon Berenguer
b: abt 1090-Spain
m: abt 1113-Spain
d: 19 Aug 1131-Barcelona, Spain

Empress Berenguela of Barcelona
b: 1116-Barcelona, Spain
d: aft 1149-Spain

Dolça de Gévaudaun
b: abt 1095-Spain
d: Spain

Chart #16

Ancestors of Queen Blanca of Navarre

Lord Ramiro Sanchez of Monzón
b: abt 1075-Spain
m: abt 1098-Spain
d: 1116-Spain

King Garcia Ramirez VII of Navarre
b: abt 1100-Navarre
m: abt 1128-Spain
d: 21 Nov 1150-Navarre

Cristina de Vivar
b: abt 1080-Spain
d: Spain

Queen Blanca of Navarre
b: abt 1135-Navarre
d: 12 Aug 1156-Toledo, Spain

Seigneur Gilbert de l'Aigle
b: abt 1085-Spain
m: abt 1108-Spain
d: Spain

Queen Marguerite de l'Aigle
b: abt 1110-France
d: 25 May 1141-Navarre

Juliane du Perche
b: abt 1090-France
d: Spain

Chart #17

Ancestors of King Philip II Augustus Capet

King Louis VI Capet
b: 1 Dec 1081-Paris, France
d: 1 Aug 1137-France

King Louis VII Capet
b: 1120-France
m: Nov 1160-France
d: 18 Sep 1180-Paris, France

Queen Adelaide of Maurienne
b: 1092-Savoy
d: 18 Nov 1154-France

King Philip II Augustus Capet
b: 21 Aug 1165-France
d: 14 Jul 1223-France

Count Thibaut of Champagne
b: 1090-Champagne, France
m: 1123-Austria
d: 8 Jan 1152-Champagne, France

Queen Adela of Champagne
b: abt 1142-Blois, France
d: 1206-Paris, France

Countess Matilda of Carinthia
b: abt 1105-Austria
d: 13 Dec 1160-Champagne, France

Chart #18

Ancestors of King Alfonso II of Aragon

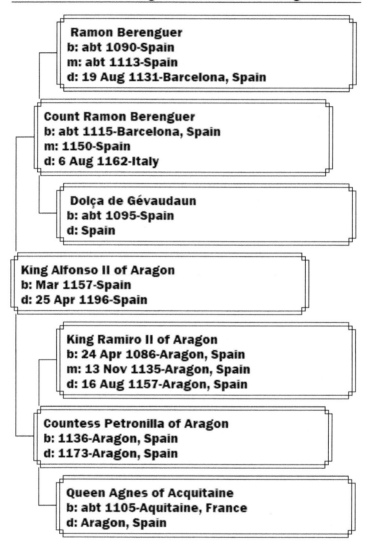

Ramon Berenguer
b: abt 1090-Spain
m: abt 1113-Spain
d: 19 Aug 1131-Barcelona, Spain

Count Ramon Berenguer
b: abt 1115-Barcelona, Spain
m: 1150-Spain
d: 6 Aug 1162-Italy

Dolça de Gévaudaun
b: abt 1095-Spain
d: Spain

King Alfonso II of Aragon
b: Mar 1157-Spain
d: 25 Apr 1196-Spain

King Ramiro II of Aragon
b: 24 Apr 1086-Aragon, Spain
m: 13 Nov 1135-Aragon, Spain
d: 16 Aug 1157-Aragon, Spain

Countess Petronilla of Aragon
b: 1136-Aragon, Spain
d: 1173-Aragon, Spain

Queen Agnes of Acquitaine
b: abt 1105-Aquitaine, France
d: Aragon, Spain

Chart #19

Ancestors of Queen Sanchia of Castile

Count Raymond of Spain
b: 1070-Burgundy, France
d: Sep 1107-Spain

Emperor Alfonso VII of Spain
b: 1 Mar 1105-Spain
m: bef 25 Nov 1152-Spain
d: 21 Aug 1157-Spain

Countess Urraca of Castile
b: 1081-Castile, Spain
d: 10 Mar 1126-Castile, Spain

Queen Sanchia of Castile
b: 21 Sep 1154-Spain
d: Nov 1208-Spain

King Wladyslaw II Wrymouth of Poland
b: abt 1105-Poland
d: 30 May 1159-Poland

Empress Richeza of Poland
b: abt 1135-Poland
d: 16 Jun 1185-Germany

Queen Agnes of Babengerg
b: abt 1115-Austria
d: aft 1146-Poland

Chart #20

Ancestors of King Bela III of Hungary

King Bela II of Hungary The Blind
b: 1105-Hungary
m: by 1129-Hungary
d: 13 Feb 1141-Hungary

King Geza II of Hungary
b: 1130-Hungary
m: 1146-Kiev
d: 31 May 1162-Hungary

Queen Helen of Rascia
b: abt 1110-Russia
d: aft 1146-Hungary

King Bela III of Hungary
b: abt 1150-Hungary
d: 23 Apr 1196-Hungary

Mstislav Vladimiravich of Novgorod
b: abt 1105-Russia
d: Kiev

Queen Euphrosyne of Kiev
b: abt 1130-Kiev
d: Hungary

Princess Cristina Ingesdotter of Sweden
b: abt 1110-Sweden
d: Kiev

Chart #21

Ancestors of Emperor Peter II de Courtenay

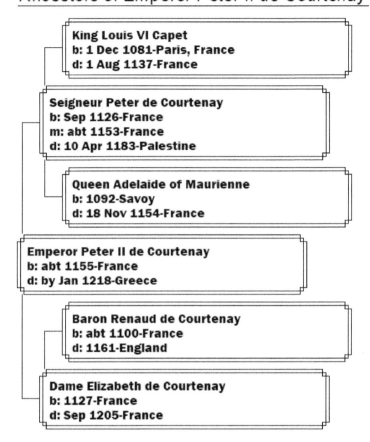

King Louis VI Capet
b: 1 Dec 1081-Paris, France
d: 1 Aug 1137-France

Seigneur Peter de Courtenay
b: Sep 1126-France
m: abt 1153-France
d: 10 Apr 1183-Palestine

Queen Adelaide of Maurienne
b: 1092-Savoy
d: 18 Nov 1154-France

Emperor Peter II de Courtenay
b: abt 1155-France
d: by Jan 1218-Greece

Baron Renaud de Courtenay
b: abt 1100-France
d: 1161-England

Dame Elizabeth de Courtenay
b: 1127-France
d: Sep 1205-France

Chart #22

Ancestors of Queen Matilda of Flanders

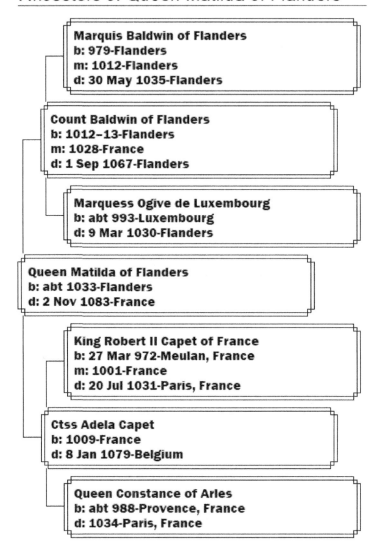

Marquis Baldwin of Flanders
b: 979-Flanders
m: 1012-Flanders
d: 30 May 1035-Flanders

Count Baldwin of Flanders
b: 1012–13-Flanders
m: 1028-France
d: 1 Sep 1067-Flanders

Marquess Ogive de Luxembourg
b: abt 993-Luxembourg
d: 9 Mar 1030-Flanders

Queen Matilda of Flanders
b: abt 1033-Flanders
d: 2 Nov 1083-France

King Robert II Capet of France
b: 27 Mar 972-Meulan, France
m: 1001-France
d: 20 Jul 1031-Paris, France

Ctss Adela Capet
b: 1009-France
d: 8 Jan 1079-Belgium

Queen Constance of Arles
b: abt 988-Provence, France
d: 1034-Paris, France

Chart #23

Ancestors of King Malcolm III of Scotland

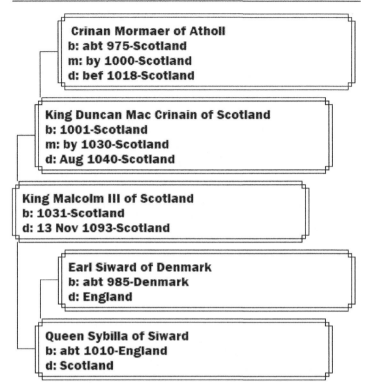

Crinan Mormaer of Atholl
b: abt 975-Scotland
m: by 1000-Scotland
d: bef 1018-Scotland

King Duncan Mac Crinain of Scotland
b: 1001-Scotland
m: by 1030-Scotland
d: Aug 1040-Scotland

King Malcolm III of Scotland
b: 1031-Scotland
d: 13 Nov 1093-Scotland

Earl Siward of Denmark
b: abt 985-Denmark
d: England

Queen Sybilla of Siward
b: abt 1010-England
d: Scotland

Chart #24

Ancestors of Saint Margaret of Hungary

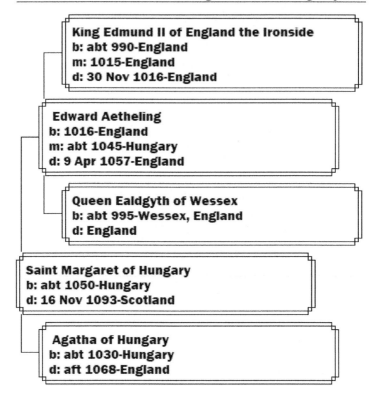

King Edmund II of England the Ironside
b: abt 990-England
m: 1015-England
d: 30 Nov 1016-England

Edward Aetheling
b: 1016-England
m: abt 1045-Hungary
d: 9 Apr 1057-England

Queen Ealdgyth of Wessex
b: abt 995-Wessex, England
d: England

Saint Margaret of Hungary
b: abt 1050-Hungary
d: 16 Nov 1093-Scotland

Agatha of Hungary
b: abt 1030-Hungary
d: aft 1068-England

Chart #25

Ancestors of King Alfonso VI of Castile & Leon

King Sancho III of Navarre
b: abt 995-Navarre
m: abt 1015-Spain
d: 18 Oct 1035-Navarre

King Fernando I of Castile and Leon
b: 1016–18-Navarre
m: Dec 1032-Spain
d: 27 Dec 1065-Spain

Queen Munia Mayor de Castilla
b: abt 995-Castile, Spain
d: 1066-Spain

King Alfonso VI of Castile & Leon
b: 1038–40-Castile, Spain
d: 1 Jul 1109-Castile, Spain

King Alfonso V de León
b: abt 995-Spain
m: abt 1015-Spain
d: Aug 1028-Spain

Queen Sanchia de León
b: abt 1017-Spain
d: 7 Nov 1067-Spain

Queen Elvira Menendez
b: abt 997-Spain
d: 2 Dec 1022-Spain

Chart #26

Ancestors of Queen Constance of Burgundy

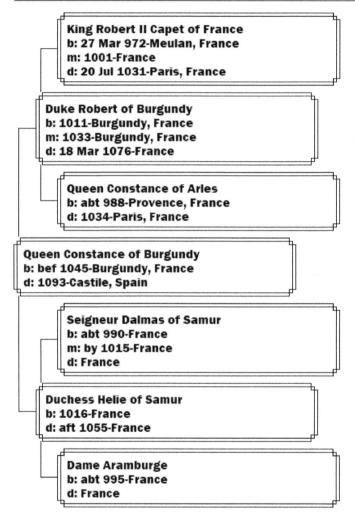

King Robert II Capet of France
b: 27 Mar 972-Meulan, France
m: 1001-France
d: 20 Jul 1031-Paris, France

Duke Robert of Burgundy
b: 1011-Burgundy, France
m: 1033-Burgundy, France
d: 18 Mar 1076-France

Queen Constance of Arles
b: abt 988-Provence, France
d: 1034-Paris, France

Queen Constance of Burgundy
b: bef 1045-Burgundy, France
d: 1093-Castile, Spain

Seigneur Dalmas of Samur
b: abt 990-France
m: by 1015-France
d: France

Duchess Helie of Samur
b: 1016-France
d: aft 1055-France

Dame Aramburge
b: abt 995-France
d: France

Chart #27

Ancestors of King Louis VI Capet

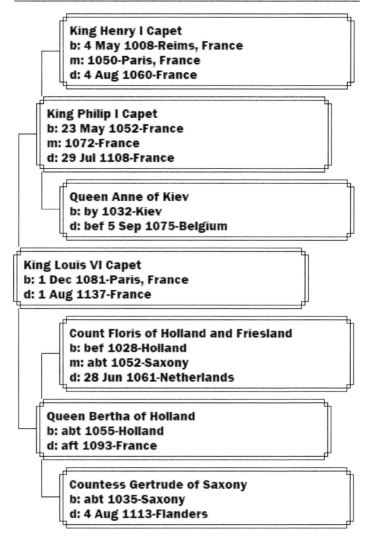

King Henry I Capet
b: 4 May 1008-Reims, France
m: 1050-Paris, France
d: 4 Aug 1060-France

King Philip I Capet
b: 23 May 1052-France
m: 1072-France
d: 29 Jul 1108-France

Queen Anne of Kiev
b: by 1032-Kiev
d: bef 5 Sep 1075-Belgium

King Louis VI Capet
b: 1 Dec 1081-Paris, France
d: 1 Aug 1137-France

Count Floris of Holland and Friesland
b: bef 1028-Holland
m: abt 1052-Saxony
d: 28 Jun 1061-Netherlands

Queen Bertha of Holland
b: abt 1055-Holland
d: aft 1093-France

Countess Gertrude of Saxony
b: abt 1035-Saxony
d: 4 Aug 1113-Flanders

Chart #28

Ancestors of Queen Agnes of Babengerg

Margrave Leopold of Austria
b: 1050-Austria
d: 12 Oct 1095-Austria

Saint Leopold III of Austria
b: 1073-Austria
m: 1106-Austria
d: 24 Sep 1143-Austria

Queen Agnes of Babengerg
b: abt 1115-Austria
d: aft 1146-Poland

Emperor Henry IV Hohenstaufen
b: 11 Nov 1050-Saxony
m: 1066-Savoy
d: 7 Aug 1106-Lorraine

Duchess Agnes Hohenstaufen
b: 1072–73-Germany
d: 24 Sep 1143-Austria

Empress Bertha of Savoy
b: abt 1052-Savoy
d: by 1089-Germany

Chart #29

Ancestors of King Robert II Capet of France

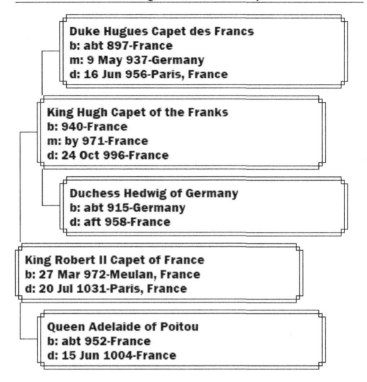

Duke Hugues Capet des Francs
b: abt 897-France
m: 9 May 937-Germany
d: 16 Jun 956-Paris, France

King Hugh Capet of the Franks
b: 940-France
m: by 971-France
d: 24 Oct 996-France

Duchess Hedwig of Germany
b: abt 915-Germany
d: aft 958-France

King Robert II Capet of France
b: 27 Mar 972-Meulan, France
d: 20 Jul 1031-Paris, France

Queen Adelaide of Poitou
b: abt 952-France
d: 15 Jun 1004-France

Chart #30

Ancestors of King Edmund II of England

King Edgar of England the Peaceful
b: abt 935-England
m: abt 958-England
d: 8 Jul 975-England

King Æthelred II of England the Unready
b: abt 960-England
m: abt 983-England
d: 23 Apr 1016-England

Queen Aelthryth Ordgar
b: abt 940-England
d: England

King Edmund II of England
b: abt 990-England
d: 30 Nov 1016-England

Earl Thored of Northumbria
b: abt 940-Northumberland, England
d: Northumberland, England

Queen Aelfgifu of Northumbria
b: abt 965-Northumberland, England
d: by 1002-England

Chart #31

Ancestors of King Henry I Capet

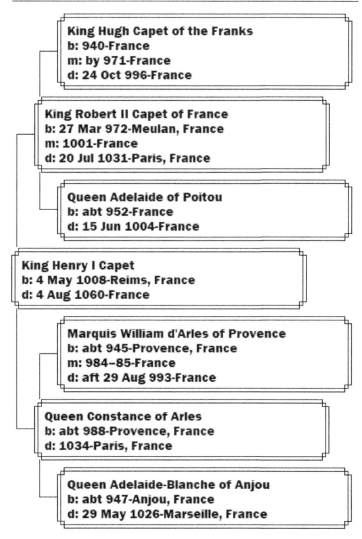

King Hugh Capet of the Franks
b: 940-France
m: by 971-France
d: 24 Oct 996-France

King Robert II Capet of France
b: 27 Mar 972-Meulan, France
m: 1001-France
d: 20 Jul 1031-Paris, France

Queen Adelaide of Poitou
b: abt 952-France
d: 15 Jun 1004-France

King Henry I Capet
b: 4 May 1008-Reims, France
d: 4 Aug 1060-France

Marquis William d'Arles of Provence
b: abt 945-Provence, France
m: 984–85-France
d: aft 29 Aug 993-France

Queen Constance of Arles
b: abt 988-Provence, France
d: 1034-Paris, France

Queen Adelaide-Blanche of Anjou
b: abt 947-Anjou, France
d: 29 May 1026-Marseille, France

Chart #32

Ancestors of Queen Anne of Kiev

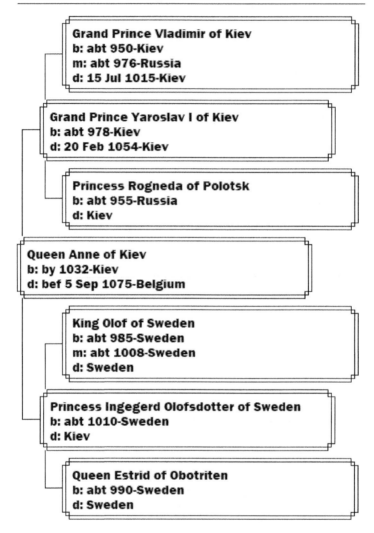

Grand Prince Vladimir of Kiev
b: abt 950-Kiev
m: abt 976-Russia
d: 15 Jul 1015-Kiev

Grand Prince Yaroslav I of Kiev
b: abt 978-Kiev
d: 20 Feb 1054-Kiev

Princess Rogneda of Polotsk
b: abt 955-Russia
d: Kiev

Queen Anne of Kiev
b: by 1032-Kiev
d: bef 5 Sep 1075-Belgium

King Olof of Sweden
b: abt 985-Sweden
m: abt 1008-Sweden
d: Sweden

Princess Ingegerd Olofsdotter of Sweden
b: abt 1010-Sweden
d: Kiev

Queen Estrid of Obotriten
b: abt 990-Sweden
d: Sweden

Chart #33

Ancestors of Emperor Henry IV Hohenstaufen

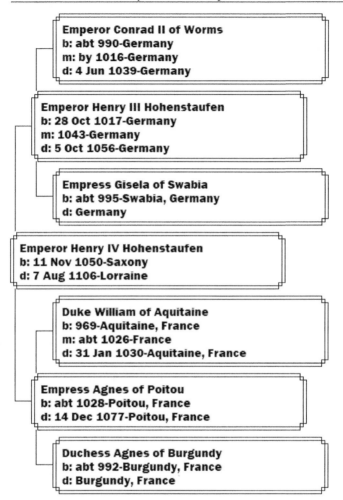

Emperor Conrad II of Worms
b: abt 990-Germany
m: by 1016-Germany
d: 4 Jun 1039-Germany

Emperor Henry III Hohenstaufen
b: 28 Oct 1017-Germany
m: 1043-Germany
d: 5 Oct 1056-Germany

Empress Gisela of Swabia
b: abt 995-Swabia, Germany
d: Germany

Emperor Henry IV Hohenstaufen
b: 11 Nov 1050-Saxony
d: 7 Aug 1106-Lorraine

Duke William of Aquitaine
b: 969-Aquitaine, France
m: abt 1026-France
d: 31 Jan 1030-Aquitaine, France

Empress Agnes of Poitou
b: abt 1028-Poitou, France
d: 14 Dec 1077-Poitou, France

Duchess Agnes of Burgundy
b: abt 992-Burgundy, France
d: Burgundy, France

Chart #34

Ancestors of Queen Margaret of Norway

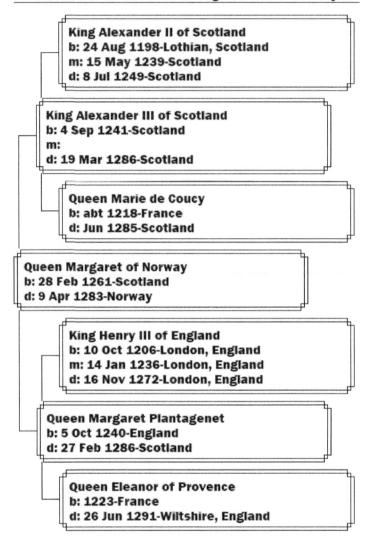

King Alexander II of Scotland
b: 24 Aug 1198-Lothian, Scotland
m: 15 May 1239-Scotland
d: 8 Jul 1249-Scotland

King Alexander III of Scotland
b: 4 Sep 1241-Scotland
m:
d: 19 Mar 1286-Scotland

Queen Marie de Coucy
b: abt 1218-France
d: Jun 1285-Scotland

Queen Margaret of Norway
b: 28 Feb 1261-Scotland
d: 9 Apr 1283-Norway

King Henry III of England
b: 10 Oct 1206-London, England
m: 14 Jan 1236-London, England
d: 16 Nov 1272-London, England

Queen Margaret Plantagenet
b: 5 Oct 1240-England
d: 27 Feb 1286-Scotland

Queen Eleanor of Provence
b: 1223-France
d: 26 Jun 1291-Wiltshire, England

Chart #35
Ancestors of King William of Scotland

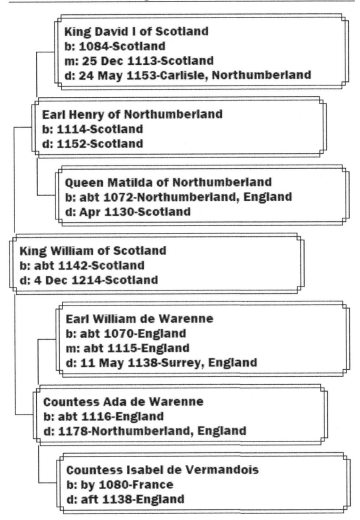

King David I of Scotland
b: 1084-Scotland
m: 25 Dec 1113-Scotland
d: 24 May 1153-Carlisle, Northumberland

Earl Henry of Northumberland
b: 1114-Scotland
d: 1152-Scotland

Queen Matilda of Northumberland
b: abt 1072-Northumberland, England
d: Apr 1130-Scotland

King William of Scotland
b: abt 1142-Scotland
d: 4 Dec 1214-Scotland

Earl William de Warenne
b: abt 1070-England
m: abt 1115-England
d: 11 May 1138-Surrey, England

Countess Ada de Warenne
b: abt 1116-England
d: 1178-Northumberland, England

Countess Isabel de Vermandois
b: by 1080-France
d: aft 1138-England

Chart #36
Ancestors of King Stephen V of Hungary

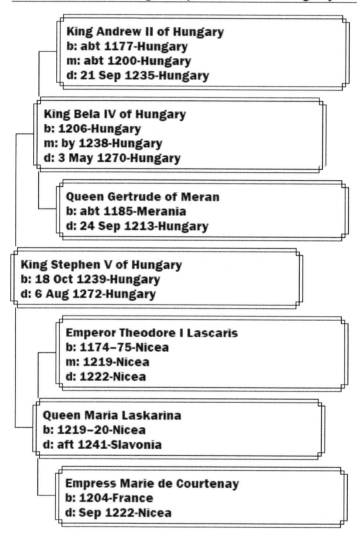

King Andrew II of Hungary
b: abt 1177-Hungary
m: abt 1200-Hungary
d: 21 Sep 1235-Hungary

King Bela IV of Hungary
b: 1206-Hungary
m: by 1238-Hungary
d: 3 May 1270-Hungary

Queen Gertrude of Meran
b: abt 1185-Merania
d: 24 Sep 1213-Hungary

King Stephen V of Hungary
b: 18 Oct 1239-Hungary
d: 6 Aug 1272-Hungary

Emperor Theodore I Lascaris
b: 1174–75-Nicea
m: 1219-Nicea
d: 1222-Nicea

Queen Maria Laskarina
b: 1219–20-Nicea
d: aft 1241-Slavonia

Empress Marie de Courtenay
b: 1204-France
d: Sep 1222-Nicea

Descendent Lists for Four Generations

Explanation of generational markings:

Notation used before a descendancy chart.

>>>... The history of this royal family can be found in the book of this series on the early history of **England**, which begins in 54 B.C.

///... The history of this royal family can be found in the book of this series on the early history of **France**, which begins in 58 B.C.

###... The history of this royal family can be found in the book of this series on the early history of **Spain**, which begins in 800A.D.

***... The history of this royal family is found **only** in this book.

>>>
1-King Louis IX OF FRANCE (husband)
+Queen Marguerite OF PROVENCE (wife)
❖ **2-King Philip III OF FRANCE (son)**
❖ **+Queen Isabella OF ARAGON (son's 1st wife)**
  • 3-King Philip IV OF FRANCE (grandson)
  • +Queen Jeanne OF NAVARRE (his wife)
    o 4-King Louis X OF FRANCE (great grandson)
❖ **+Queen Marie OF BRABANT (son's 2nd wife)**

>>>

1-King Edward III OF ENGLAND (1312-1377)
+Queen Philippa OF HAUNAULT (1311-1369)
❖ **2-Duke Lionel OF ANTWERP (1338-1368)**
❖ +Duchess Elizabeth DE BURGH (1332-1363)
  - 3-Lady Philippe OF CLARENCE (1355-1377)
  - +Earl Edmund DE MORTIMER (1351-1381)
    - ○ 4-Elizabeth DE MORTIMER (1370-1417)
❖ **2-Duke John OF GAUNT (1340-1399)**
❖ **+Katherine DE ROET (1350-1403)**
  - 3-Marquess John BEAUFORT (1373-1410)
  - +Duchess Margaret HOLLAND (1385-1439)
    - ○ 4-Duke John BEAUFORT (1404-1444)
    - ○ 4-Duke Edmund BEAUFORT (1406-1455)
  - 3-Countess Joan BEAUFORT (1377-1437)
  - +Earl Ralph DE NEVILLE (1364-1425)
    - ○ 4-Earl Richard NEVILLE (1400-1461)
    - ○ +Blanche PLANTAGENET (1341-1368)
  - 3-King Henry IV (1367-1413)
❖ **2-Duke Thomas OF WOODSTOCK (1355-1397)**
❖ **+Duchess Eleanor DE BOHUN (1362-1399)**
  - 3-Countess Anne OF WOODSTOCK (1383-1438)
  - +Count William BOURCHIER (1374-1420)
    - ○ 4-Lord John BOURGCHIER (1415-1474)

\>\>\>

1-King Edward I OF ENGLAND (1239-1307)
+Queen Eleanor OF CASTILE (1241-1290)
❖ 2-Countess Joan OF ACRE (1272-1307)
❖ +Earl Gilbert DE CLARE (1243-1295)
- 3-Eleanor DE CLARE (1292-1337)
- +Lord Hugh LE DESPENSER the younger (1285-1326)
  o 4-Isabel LE DESPENSER (1313-1356)
  o 4-Elizabeth LE DESPENSER (1325-1389)
- 3-Countess Margaret DE CLARE (1293-1342)
- +Earl Hugh DE AUDLEY (1289-1347)
  o 4-Countess Margaret DE AUDLEY (1320-1357)
- 3-Lady Elizabeth DE CLARE (1295-1360)
- +Theobaud DE VERDUN (1278-1316)
  o 4-Isabel DE VERDUN (1317-1349)
  o +Sir John DE BURGH (1280-1313)
  o 4-Earl William DE BURGH (1312-1333)
  o +Lord Roger DE AMORY (1285-1322)
  o 4-Elizabeth D'AMORIE (1318-1361)
  o +Earl Ralph DE MONTHERMER (1262-1325)
- 3-Lord Thomas DE MONTHERMER (1301-1340)
- +Dame Margaret DE BREWES (1310-1349)
  o 4-Margaret DE MONTHERMER (1329-1395)
❖ 2-Countess Elizabeth OF WALES (1282-1316)
❖ +Earl Humphrey DE BOHUN (1276-1322)
- 3-Countess Margaret DE BOHUN (1311-1391)
- +Earl Hugh DE COURTENAY (1303-1377)
  o 4-Sir Edward DE COURTENAY (1331-1370)
  o 4-Margaret COURTENAY (1350-)
  o 4-Admiral Philip DE COURTENAY (1355-1406)
- 3-Earl William DE BOHUN (1312-1360)
- +Countess Elizabeth DE BADLESMERE (1312-1356)
  o 4-Countess Elizabeth DE BOHUN (1336-1385)
  o 4-Earl Humphrey DE BOHUN (1341-1373)

- ❖ **2-King Edward II OF ENGLAND (1284-1327)**
- ❖ **+Queen Isabella OF FRANCE (1295-1358)**
  - • 3-King Edward III OF ENGLAND (1312-1377)
  - • +Queen Philippa OF HAUNAULT (1311-1369)
    - ○ 4-Duke Lionel OF ANTWERP (1338-1368)
    - ○ 4-Duke John OF GAUNT (1340-1399)
    - ○ 4-Duke Thomas OF WOODSTOCK (1355-1397)

+Queen Marguerite OF FRANCE (1282-1318)
- ❖ **2-Earl Thomas OF BROTHERTON (1300-1338)**
- ❖ **+Countess Alice HAYLES (1295-1330)**
  - • 3-Margaret PLANTAGENET (1319-1399)
  - • +Baron John DE SEGRAVE (1315-1353)
    - ○ 4-Elizabeth SEAGRAVE (1338-1376)
- ❖ **2-Earl Edmund OF WOODSTOCK (1301-1330)**
- ❖ **+Countess Margaret WAKE (1300-1349)**
  - • 3-Countess Joan OF KENT (1328-1385)
  - • +Earl Thomas DE HOLAND (1314-1360)
    - ○ 4-Earl Thomas DE HOLAND (1350-1397)
  - • +Prince Edward OF WOODSTOCK (1330-1376)
    - ○ 4-King Richard II of England (1367-1399)

///
1-King Philip IV OF FRANCE (1268-1314)
+Queen Jeanne OF NAVARRE (1273-1305)
- ❖ **2-King Louis X OF FRANCE (1289-1316)**
- ❖ **2-King Philip V OF FRANCE (1292-1322)**
- ❖ **2-King Charles IV OF FRANCE (1294-1322)**
- ❖ **2-Queen Isabella OF FRANCE (1295-1358)**
- ❖ **+King Edward II OF ENGLAND (1284-1327)**
  - 3-King Edward III OF ENGLAND (1312-1377)
  - +Queen Philippa OF HAUNAULT (1311-1369)
    - ○ 4-Prince Edward OF WOODSTOCK (1330-1376)
    - ○ 4-Duke Lionel OF ANTWERP (1338-1368)
    - ○ 4-Duke John OF GAUNT (1340-1399)
    - ○ 4-Duke Thomas OF WOODSTOCK (1355-1397)
  - 3-Queen Joan OF THE TOWER (1321-1362)
  - +King David II OF SCOTLAND (1324-1371)

>>>
1-King John OF ENGLAND (1166-1216)
+Queen Isabella OF ANGOULEME (1188-1246)
❖ **2-King Henry III OF ENGLAND (1206-1272)**
❖ **+Queen Eleanor OF PROVENCE (1223-1291)**
- 3-King Edward I OF ENGLAND (1239-1307)
- +Queen Eleanor OF CASTILE (1241-1290)
  - 4-Countess Joan OF ACRE (1272-1307)
  - 4-Countess Elizabeth OF WALES (1282-1316)
  - 4-King Edward II OF ENGLAND (1284-1327)
- +Queen Marguerite OF FRANCE (1282-1318)
  - 4-Earl Thomas OF BROTHERTON (1300-1338)
  - 4-Earl Edmund OF WOODSTOCK (1301-1330)
- 3-Queen Margaret PLANTAGENET (1240-1286)
- +King Alexander III OF SCOTLAND (1241-1286)
  - 4-Queen Margaret OF NORWAY (1261-1283)
- 3-Earl Edmund OF LANCASTER (1244-1296)
- +Queen Blanche OF ARTOIS (1248-1302)
  - 4-Earl Henry OF LANCASTER (1281-1345)

❖ **2-King Richard OF CORNWALL (1209-1272)**
❖ **+Joan VALLETORT (1230-)**
- 3-Sir Richard OF CORNWALL (1255-1296)
- +Joan FITZ ALLEYN (1270-1319)
  - 4-Joan OF CORNWALL (1290-1342)
- 3-Joanna VALLETORT (1260-1319)
- +Richard DE CHAMBERNOUN (1250-1300)
  - 4-Lord Richard DE CHAMPERNOUN (1292-1338)
- 3-Lord Walter OF CORNWALL (1253-1313)
- +Margery "of Cornwall" (1265-)
  - 4-Sir William DE CORNWALL (1286-1343)
  - 4-Margaret OF CORNWALL (1290-1349)

###
1-King Alfonso IX OF LEON (1171-1230)
+Queen Berenguela OF CASTILE (1181-1246)
❖ **2-King Fernando III OF CASTILE (1199-1252)**
❖ **+Queen Jeanne DE DAMMARTIN (1219-1279)**
  - 3-Queen Eleanor OF CASTILE (1241-1290)
  - +King Edward I OF ENGLAND (1239-1307)
    - ○ 4-Countess Joan OF ACRE (1272-1307)
    - ○ 4-Countess Elizabeth OF WALES (1282-1316)
    - ○ 4-King Edward II OF ENGLAND (1284-1327)
❖ **2-Empress Berengere OF CASTILE-LEON (1204-1246)**
❖ **+Emperor Jean DE BRIENNE (1170-1237)**
  - 3-Sir Jean "dit A'rce" DE BRIENNE (1229-1296)
  - +Jeanne DE CHATEAUDUN (1230-1253)
    - ○ 4-Blanche DE BRIENNE (1252-1302)
  - 3-Vicomte Louis DE BRIENNE (1231-1297)
  - +Lady Agnes DE BEAUMONT (1230-1304)
    - ○ 4-Earl Henry DE BEAUMONT (1270-1340)

///

1-King Louis IX OF FRANCE (1214-1270)
+Queen Marguerite OF PROVENCE (1221-1295)

❖ **2-King Philip III OF FRANCE (1245-1285)**
❖ **+Queen Isabella OF ARAGON (1251-1271)**
- 3-King Philip IV OF FRANCE (1268-1314)
- +Queen Jeanne OF NAVARRE (1273-1305)
  - o 4-King Louis X OF FRANCE (1289-1316)
  - o 4-King Philip V OF FRANCE (1292-1322)
  - o 4-King Charles IV OF FRANCE (1294-1322)
  - o 4-Queen Isabella OF FRANCE (1295-1358)
- 3-Count Charles OF VALOIS (1270-1325)
- +Countess Margaret OF NAPLES (1273-1299)
  - o 4-Countess Jeanne OF VALOIS (1293-1342)
❖ **+Queen Marie OF BRABANT (1254-1321)**
- 3-Queen Marguerite OF FRANCE (1282-1318)
- +King Edward I OF ENGLAND (1239-1307)
  - o 4-Earl Thomas OF BROTHERTON (1300-1338)
  - o 4-Earl Edmund OF WOODSTOCK (1301-1330)

###
1-King James I OF ARAGON (1208-1276)
+Queen Yolande OF HUNGARY (1216-1251)
❖ **2-Queen Isabella OF ARAGON (1251-1271)**
❖ **+King Philip III OF FRANCE (1245-1285)**
- 3-King Philip IV OF FRANCE (1268-1314)
- +Queen Jeanne OF NAVARRE (1273-1305)
  - o 4-King Louis X OF FRANCE (1289-1316)
  - o 4-King Philip V OF FRANCE (1292-1322)
  - o 4-King Charles IV OF FRANCE (1294-1322)
  - o 4-Queen Isabella OF FRANCE (1295-1358)
- 3-Count Charles OF VALOIS (1270-1325)
- +Countess Margaret OF NAPLES (1273-1299)
  - o 4-Countess Jeanne OF VALOIS (1293-1342)

>>>
1-Empress Matilda FITZ ROY (1102-1167)
+Comte Geoffrey PLANTAGENET (1113-1151)
❖ **2-King Henry II OF ENGLAND (1133-1189)**
❖ **+Queen Eleanor OF AQUITAINE (1122-1204)**
- 3-King Henry the Young OF ENGLAND (1155-1183)
- 3-King Richard I OF ENGLAND (1157-1199)
- 3-Queen Eleanor PLANTAGENET (1162-1214)
- +King Alfonso VIII OF CASTILE (1155-1214)
  - 4-Queen Berenguela OF CASTILE (1181-1246)
  - 4-Queen Blanche OF CASTILE (1188-1252)
- 3-King John OF ENGLAND (1166-1216)
- +Queen Isabella OF ANGOULEME (1188-1246)
  - 4-King Henry III OF ENGLAND (1206-1272)
  - 4-King Richard OF CORNWALL (1209-1272)

###

1-Emperor Alfonso VII of Spain (1105-1157)
+Empress Berenguela OF BARCELONA (1116-1149)
- ❖ **2-King Sancho III OF CASTILE (1134-1158)**
- ❖ **+Queen Blanca OF NAVARRE (1135-1156)**
  - • 3-King Alfonso VIII OF CASTILE (1155-1214)
  - • +Queen Eleanor PLANTAGENET (1162-1214)
    - ○ 4-Queen Berenguela OF CASTILE (1181-1246)
    - ○ 4-Queen Blanche OF CASTILE (1188-1252)
- ❖ **2-Queen Sancha OF CASTILE (1136-1179)**
- ❖ **+King Sancho VI OF NAVARRE (1130-1194)**
  - • 3-Comtesse Blanche OF NAVARRE (1179-1229)
  - • +Comte Thibaut "III" OF CHAMPAGNE (1181-1201)
    - ○ 4-King Thibaut OF NAVARRE IV of Champagne (1201-1253)
- ❖ **2-King Ferdinand II OF LEON (1137-1188)**
- ❖ **+Queen Urraca OF PORTUGAL (1148-1211)**
  - • 3-King Alfonso IX OF LEON (1171-1230)
  - • +Queen Berenguela OF CASTILE (1181-1246)
    - ○ 4-King Fernando III OF CASTILE (1199-1252)
    - ○ 4-Empress Berengere OF CASTILE-LEON (1204-1246)
- ❖ **2-Queen Constance OF CASTILE (1141-1160)**
- ❖ **+King Louis VII CAPET (1120-1180)**
  - • 3-Comtesse Alais DE CAPET (1160-1218)
  - • +Comte William DE MONTGOMERIE (1179-1221)
    - ○ 4-Countess Marie OF PONTHIEU (1199-1250)

+Empress Richeza OF POLAND (1135-1185)
- ❖ **2-Queen Sanchia OF CASTILE (1154-1208)**
- ❖ **+King Alfonso II of Aragon (1157-1196)**
  - 3-King Pedro II OF ARAGON (1176-1213)
  - +Queen Marie OF MONTPELLIER (1182-1213)
    - ○ 4-King James I OF ARAGON (1208-1276)
  - 3-Conde Alfonso II OF PROVENCE (1177-1209)
  - +Condesa Garsenda OF SABRAN (1175-)
    - ○ 4-Count Raymond IV BERENGAR (1195-1245)

###
1-King Alfonso OF PORTUGAL (1109-1185)
+Queen Mafalda OF SAVOY (1125-1196)
❖ **2-Queen Urraca OF PORTUGAL (1148-1211)**
❖ **+King Ferdinand II OF LEON (1137-1188)**
- 3-King Alfonso IX OF LEON (1171-1230)
- +Queen Berenguela OF CASTILE (1181-1246)
  - ○ 4-King Fernando III OF CASTILE (1199-1252)
  - ○ 4-Empress Berengere OF CASTILE-LEON (1204-1246)

\#\#\#
1-King Sancho III OF CASTILE (1134-1158)
+Queen Blanca OF NAVARRE (1135-1156)
❖ **2-King Alfonso VIII OF CASTILE (1155-1214)**
❖ **+Queen Eleanor PLANTAGENET (1162-1214)**
- 3-Queen Berenguela OF CASTILE (1181-1246)
- +King Alfonso IX OF LEON (1171-1230)
  - ○ 4-King Fernando III OF CASTILE (1199-1252)
  - ○ 4-Empress Berengere OF CASTILE-LEON (1204-1246)
- 3-Queen Blanche OF CASTILE (1188-1252)
- +King Louis VIII CAPET (1187-1226)
  - ○ 4-King Louis IX OF FRANCE (1214-1270)
  - ○ 4-Count Robert OF ARTOIS (1216-1250)
  - ○ 4-King Charles "I" OF NAPLES (1226-1285)

///
1-King Philip II AUGUSTUS Capet (1165-1223)
+Queen Isabelle OF HAINAUT (1170-1190)
❖ **2-King Louis VIII CAPET (1187-1226)**
❖ **+Queen Blanche OF CASTILE (1188-1252)**
- 3-King Louis IX OF FRANCE (1214-1270)
- +Queen Marguerite OF PROVENCE (1221-1295)
  - 4-King Philip III OF FRANCE (1245-1285)
- 3-Count Robert OF ARTOIS (1216-1250)
- +Countess Matilda OF BRABANT (1224-1288)
  - 4-Queen Blanche OF ARTOIS (1248-1302)
- 3-King Charles "I" OF NAPLES (1226-1285)
- +Queen Beatrice OF PROVENCE (1230-1267)
  - 4-King Charles II OF NAPLES (1254-1309)

###
1-King Alfonso II of Aragon (1157-1196)
+Queen Sanchia OF CASTILE (1154-1208)
- ❖ 2-King Pedro II OF ARAGON (1176-1213)
- ❖ +Queen Marie OF MONTPELLIER (1182-1213)
  - 3-King James I OF ARAGON (1208-1276)
  - +Queen Yolande OF HUNGARY (1216-1251)
    - ○ 4-Queen Isabella OF ARAGON (1251-1271)
- ❖ 2-Conde Alfonso II OF PROVENCE (1177-1209)
- ❖ +Condesa Garsenda OF SABRAN (1175-)
  - 3-Count Raymond IV BERENGAR (1195-1245)
  - +Countess Beatrice OF SAVOIA (1207-1265)
    - ○ 4-Queen Marguerite OF PROVENCE (1221-1295)
    - ○ 4-Queen Eleanor OF PROVENCE (1223-1291)
    - ○ 4-Queen Beatrice OF PROVENCE (1230-1267)

***

1-King Bela III OF HUNGARY (1150-1196)
- ❖ **2-King Andrew II OF HUNGARY (1177-1235)**
- ❖ **+Queen Yolande DE COURTENAY (1198-1233)**
  - 3-Queen Yolande OF HUNGARY (1216-1251)
  - +King James I OF ARAGON (1208-1276)
    - ○ 4-Queen Isabella OF ARAGON (1251-1271)
    - ○ +Queen Gertrude OF MERAN (1185-1213)
  - 3-King Bela IV OF HUNGARY (1206-1270)
  - +Queen Maria LASKARINA (1219-1241)
    - ○ 4-King Stephen V OF HUNGARY (1239-1272)

***

1-Emperor Peter II DE COURTENAY (1155-1218)
+Empress Yolanda OF FLANDERS (1175-1219)
- ❖ **2-Queen Yolande DE COURTENAY (1198-1233)**
- ❖ **+King Andrew II OF HUNGARY (1177-1235)**
  - 3-Queen Yolande OF HUNGARY (1216-1251)
  - +King James I OF ARAGON (1208-1276)
    - ○ 4-Queen Isabella OF ARAGON (1251-1271)
- ❖ **2-Empress Marie DE COURTENAY (1204-1222)**
- ❖ **+Emperor Theodore I LASCARIS (1174-1222)**
  - 3-Queen Maria LASKARINA (1219-1241)
  - +King Bela IV OF HUNGARY (1206-1270)
    - ○ 4-King Stephen V OF HUNGARY (1239-1272)

>>>

1-Queen Matilda OF FLANDERS (1033-1083)
+King William the Conqueror OF ENGLAND (1027-1087)
- ❖ **2-King William II OF ENGLAND (1060-1100)**
- ❖ **2-Countess Adela OF NORMANDY (1067-1137)**
- ❖ **+Count Stephen-Henri OF BLOIS (1045-1102)**
  - • 3-Count William OF BLOIS (1082-1107)
  - • +Ctss Agnes DE SULLI (1085-)
    - ○ 4-Countess Margaret DE SULLI (1105-1145)
  - • 3-Count Thibaut "II" OF CHAMPAGNE (1090-1152)
  - • +Countess Matilda OF CARINTHIA (1105-1160)
    - ○ 4-Comte Henry "I" OF CHAMPAGNE (1126-1181)
    - ○ 4-Duchess Marie OF BLOIS (1128-1190)
    - ○ 4-Comtesse Agnes OF BLOIS (1140-1207)
    - ○ 4-Queen Adela OF CHAMPAGNE (1142-1206)
  - • 3-King Stephen OF ENGLAND (1092-1154)
  - • +Queen Mathilde OF BOULOGNE (1105-1152)
    - ○ 4-Countess Marie OF BOULOGNE (1133-1182)
- ❖ **2-King Henry I OF ENGLAND Beauclerc (1068-1135)**
- ❖ **+Queen Matilda OF SCOTLAND (1082-1118)**
  - • 3-Empress Matilda FITZ ROY (1102-1167)
  - • +Comte Geoffrey PLANTAGENET (1113-1151)
    - ○ 4-King Henry II OF ENGLAND (1133-1189)

***

1-King Malcolm III CAENMORE of Scotland (1031-1093)
+Saint Margaret OF HUNGARY (1050-1093)
❖ **2-King Edmund OF SCOTLAND (1070-)**
❖ **2-King Edgar OF SCOTLAND (1074-1107)**
❖ **2-King Alexander I OF SCOTLAND (1078-1124)**
❖ **2-Queen Matilda OF SCOTLAND (1082-1118)**
❖ **+King Henry I OF ENGLAND Beauclerc (1068-1135)**
  • 3-Empress Matilda FITZ ROY (1102-1167)
  • +Comte Geoffrey PLANTAGENET (1113-1151)
    ○ 4-King Henry II OF ENGLAND (1133-1189)
❖ **2-King David I OF SCOTLAND (1084-1153)**
❖ **+Queen Matilda OF NORTHUMBERLAND (1072-1130)**
  • 3-Earl Henry OF NORTHUMBERLAND (1114-1152)
  • +Countess Ada DE WARENNE (1116-1178)
    ○ 4-King Malcolm IV OF SCOTLAND (1141-1165)
    ○ 4-King William OF SCOTLAND (1142-1214)
    ○ 4-Duchess Margaret OF HUNTINGDON (1143-1201)
    ○ 4-Countess Ada OF HUNTINGDON (1146-1206)
    ○ 4-Earl David OF HUNTINGDON (1148-1219)
❖ **2-Comtesse Mary OF SCOTLAND (1087-1116)**
❖ **+Comte Eustace "III" OF BOULOGNE (1059-1125)**
  • 3-Queen Mathilde OF BOULOGNE (1105-1152)
  • +King Stephen OF ENGLAND (1092-1154)
    ○ 4-Countess Marie OF BOULOGNE (1133-1182)

+Queen Ingibioru OF NORWAY (1040-1069)
- ❖ **2-King Duncan II OF SCOTLAND (1065-1094)**
- ❖ **+Queen Ethelreda OF NORTHUMBRIA (1070-1094)**
    - 3-Earl William FITZ DUNCAN (1090-1151)
    - +Countess Adeliza DE RUMELLI (1120-1155)
        - ○ 4-Lady Amabil FITZ DUNCAN (1145-1201)

1-King Alfonso VI OF CASTILE & LEON (1038-1109)

+Mistress Jimena MUÑOZ DE GUZMÁN (1060-1128)

❖ **2-Countess Tarasia OF BIERZO (1078-1130)**
❖ **+Count Henri OF PORTUGAL (1069-1112)**
  - 3-King Alfonso OF PORTUGAL (1109-1185)
  - +Queen Mafalda OF SAVOY (1125-1196)
    - ○ 4-Queen Urraca OF PORTUGAL (1148-1211)

+Queen Constance OF BURGUNDY (1045-1093)
❖ **2-Countess Urraca OF CASTILE (1081-1126)**
❖ **+Count Raymond OF SPAIN (1070-1107)**
  - 3-Emperor Alfonso VII of Spain (1105-1157)
  - +Empress Berenguela OF BARCELONA (1116-1149)
    - ○ 4-King Sancho III OF CASTILE (1134-1158)
    - ○ 4-Queen Sancha OF CASTILE (1136-1179)
    - ○ 4-King Ferdinand II OF LEON (1137-1188)
    - ○ 4-Queen Constance OF CASTILE (1141-1160)
  - +Empress Richeza OF POLAND (1135-1185)
    - ○ 4-Queen Sanchia OF CASTILE (1154-1208)

>>>
1-King Louis VI Capet (1081-1137)
+Queen Adelaide OF MAURIENNE (1092-1154)
- ❖ **2-King Louis VII CAPET (1120-1180)**
- ❖ **+Queen Eleanor OF AQUITAINE (1122-1204)**
  - 3-Comtesse Marie CAPET (1145-1198)
  - +Comte Henry "I" OF CHAMPAGNE (1126-1181)
    - ○ 4-Empress Marie OF CHAMPAGNE (1174-1204)
    - ○ 4-Comte Thibaut "III" OF CHAMPAGNE (1181-1201)
- ❖ **+Queen Constance OF CASTILE (1141-1160)**
  - 3-Comtesse Alais DE CAPET (1160-1218)
  - +Comte William DE MONTGOMERIE (1179-1221)
    - ○ 4-Countess Marie OF PONTHIEU (1199-1250)
- ❖ **+Queen Adela OF CHAMPAGNE (1142-1206)**
  - 3-King Philip II AUGUSTUS Capet (1165-1223)
  - +Queen Isabelle OF HAINAUT (1170-1190)
    - ○ 4-King Louis VIII CAPET (1187-1226)
- ❖ **2-Comte Robert "I" OF DREUX (1125-1188)**
- ❖ **+Comtesse Agnes DE BAUDEMONT (1130-1204)**
  - 3-Comte Robert "II" DE DREUX (1154-1218)
  - +Comtesse Yolande DE COUCY (1164-1222)
    - ○ 4-Comte Robert "III" DE DREUX (1185-1234)
    - ○ 4-Duke Pierre MAUCLERC de Dreux (1186-1250)
    - ○ 4-Countess Philippa DE DREUX (1192-1242)

- ❖ **2-Seigneur Peter DE COURTENAY (1126-1183)**
- ❖ **+Dame Elizabeth DE COURTENAY (1127-1205)**
  - 3-Emperor Peter II DE COURTENAY (1155-1218)
  - +Empress Yolanda OF FLANDERS (1175-1219)
    - ○ 4-Queen Yolande DE COURTENAY (1198-1233)
    - ○ 4-Empress Marie DE COURTENAY (1204-1222)
  - 3-Comtesse Alice OF COURTENAY (1165-1215)
  - +Comte Audemar OF ANGOULEME (1160-1202)
    - ○ 4-Queen Isabella OF ANGOULEME (1188-1246)

***

1-Queen Agnes OF BABENGERG (1115-1146)
+King Wladyslaw II WRYMOUTH of Poland
(1105-1159)
❖ **2-Empress Richeza OF POLAND (1135-1185)**
❖ **+Emperor Alfonso VII of Spain (1105-1157)**
  - 3-Queen Sanchia OF CASTILE (1154-1208)
  - +King Alfonso II of Aragon (1157-1196)
    - o 4-King Pedro II OF ARAGON (1176-1213)
    - o 4-Conde Alfonso II OF PROVENCE (1177-1209)

///
1-King Robert II CAPET of France (972-1031)
+Queen Constance OF ARLES (988-1034)
- ❖ **2-King Henry I CAPET (1008-1060)**
- ❖ **+Queen Anne OF KIEV (1032-1075)**
  - 3-King Philip I CAPET (1052-1108)
  - +Queen Bertrade DE MONTFORT (1068-1117)
  - +Queen Bertha OF HOLLAND (1055-1093)
    - ○ 4-King Louis VI Capet (1081-1137)
  - 3-Comte Hugh DE VERMANDOIS (1053-1101)
  - +Ctss Adele OF VERMANDOIS (1057-1220)
    - ○ 4-Countess Isabel DE VERMANDOIS (1080-1138)
    - ○ 4-Mathilde DE VERMANDOIS (1100-)
- ❖ **2-Ctss Adela CAPET (1009-1079)**
- ❖ **+Count Baldwin "V" OF FLANDERS (1012-1067)**
  - 3-Marquis Baldwin OF MONS (1031-1070)
  - +Ctss Richilde "of Mons" (1035-1087)
    - ○ 4-Comte Baldwin "II" OF HAINAULT (1058-1098)
  - 3-Queen Matilda OF FLANDERS (1033-1083)
  - +King William the Conqueror OF ENGLAND (1027-1087)
    - ○ 4-King William II OF ENGLAND (1060-1100)
    - ○ 4-Countess Adela OF NORMANDY (1067-1137)
    - ○ 4-King Henry I OF ENGLAND Beauclerc (1068-1135)
  - 3-Count Robert "I" OF FLANDERS (1035-1093)
  - +Countess Gertrude OF SAXONY (1035-1113)
    - ○ 4-Duchess Gertrude DE FLANDRE (1072-1126)
- ❖ **2-Duke Robert "I" OF BURGUNDY (1011-1076)**
- ❖ **+Duchess Helie OF SAMUR (1016-1055)**
  - 3-Queen Constance OF BURGUNDY (1045-1093)
  - +King Alfonso VI OF CASTILE & LEON (1038-1109)
    - ○ 4-Countess Urraca OF CASTILE (1081-1126)

>>>

1-King Edmund II OF ENGLAND (990-1016)

❖ **+Queen Ealdgyth OF WESSEX (995-)**

❖ **2-Edward AETHELING (1016-1057)**

❖ **+Agatha OF HUNGARY (1030-1068)**

- 3-Saint Margaret OF HUNGARY (1050-1093)
- +King Malcolm III CAENMORE of Scotland (1031-1093)
  - o 4-King Edmund OF SCOTLAND (1070-)
  - o 4-King Edgar OF SCOTLAND (1074-1107)
  - o 4-King Alexander I OF SCOTLAND (1078-1124)
  - o 4-Queen Matilda OF SCOTLAND (1082-1118)
  - o 4-King David I OF SCOTLAND (1084-1153)
  - o 4-Comtesse Mary OF SCOTLAND (1087-1116)
- 3-'King' Edgar ATHELING (1053-1110)
  - o 4-Lady Margaret OF HUNTINGDON (1110-1164)

///
1-King Henry I CAPET (1008-1060)
+Queen Anne OF KIEV (1032-1075)
❖ **2-King Philip I CAPET (1052-1108)**
❖ **+Queen Bertrade DE MONTFORT (1068-1117)**
❖ **+Queen Bertha OF HOLLAND (1055-1093)**
- 3-King Louis VI Capet (1081-1137)
- +Queen Adelaide OF MAURIENNE (1092-1154)
  - o 4-King Louis VII CAPET (1120-1180)
  - o 4-Comte Robert "I" OF DREUX (1125-1188)
  - o 4-Seigneur Peter DE COURTENAY (1126-1183)
❖ **2-Comte Hugh DE VERMANDOIS (1053-1101)**
❖ **+Ctss Adele OF VERMANDOIS (1057-1220)**
- 3-Countess Isabel DE VERMANDOIS (1080-1138)
- +Earl Robert DE BEAUMONT (1046-1118)
  - o 4-Countess Isabel DE BEAUMONT (1096-1131)
  - o 4-Regent Robert DE BEAUMONT 'twin' (1104-1168)
  - o 4-Comte Waleran DE BEAUMONT 'twin' (1104-1166)
  - o +Earl William DE WARENNE (1070-1138)
  - o 4-Earl William DE WARENNE (1115-1148)
  - o 4-Countess Ada DE WARENNE (1116-1178)
  - o 4-Countess Gundred DE WARREN (1118-1166)
  - o 4-Baron Reginald DE WARENNE (1120-1179)
- 3-Mathilde DE VERMANDOIS (1100-)
- +Seigneur Raoul DE BEAUGENCY (1105-)
  - o 4-Domini Agnes DE BEAUGENCY (1120-1173)

///
1-Queen Anne OF KIEV (1032-1075)
+King Henry I CAPET (1008-1060)
❖ **2-King Philip I CAPET (1052-1108)**
❖ **+Queen Bertrade DE MONTFORT (1068-1117)**
❖ **+Queen Bertha OF HOLLAND (1055-1093)**
- 3-King Louis VI Capet (1081-1137)
- +Queen Adelaide OF MAURIENNE (1092-1154)
  - o 4-King Louis VII CAPET (1120-1180)
  - o 4-Comte Robert "I" OF DREUX (1125-1188)
  - o 4-Seigneur Peter DE COURTENAY (1126-1183)

❖ **2-Comte Hugh DE VERMANDOIS (1053-1101)**
❖ **+Ctss Adele OF VERMANDOIS (1057-1220)**
- 3-Countess Isabel DE VERMANDOIS (1080-1138)
- +Earl Robert DE BEAUMONT (1046-1118)
  - o 4-Countess Isabel DE BEAUMONT (1096-1131)
  - o 4-Regent Robert DE BEAUMONT 'twin' (1104-1168)
  - o 4-Comte Waleran DE BEAUMONT 'twin' (1104-1166)
- +Earl William DE WARENNE (1070-1138)
  - o 4-Earl William DE WARENNE (1115-1148)
  - o 4-Countess Ada DE WARENNE (1116-1178)
  - o 4-Countess Gundred DE WARREN (1118-1166)
  - o 4-Baron Reginald DE WARENNE (1120-1179)
- 3-Mathilde DE VERMANDOIS (1100-)
- +Seigneur Raoul DE BEAUGENCY (1105-)
  - o 4-Domini Agnes DE BEAUGENCY (1120-1173)

***

1-Emperor Henry IV HOHENSTAUFEN (1050-1106)

+Empress Bertha OF SAVOY (1052-1089)

❖ **2-Duchess Agnes HOHENSTAUFEN (1072-1143)**

❖ **+Duke Frederick "I" VON BUREN of Swabia (1050-1105)**

- 3-Duke Frederick II HOHENSTAUFEN (1090-1147)
- +Duchess Judith OF BAVARIA (1102-1131)
  - ○ 4-Duchess Bertha VON HOHENSTAUFEN (1122-1194)
  - ○ 4-Emperor Frederick I BARBAROSAI (1125-1190)

❖ **+Saint Leopold III OF AUSTRIA (1073-1143)**

- 3-Queen Agnes OF BABENGERG (1115-1146)
- +King Wladyslaw II WRYMOUTH of Poland (1105-1159)
  - ○ 4-Empress Richeza OF POLAND (1135-1185)

***
1-King William OF SCOTLAND (1142-1214)
+Mistress Isabel AVENELL (1157-)
❖ **2-Isabela OF SCOTLAND (1175-1225)**
❖ **+Baron Robert DE ROOS (1172-1226)**
- 3-Baron William DE ROOS (1200-1258)
- +Lucy FITZ PETER (1207-1266)
  - ○ 4-Baron Robert DE ROOS (1225-1285)
  - ○ 4-Sir William DE ROOS (1240-1310)
  - ○ 4-Alice DE ROOS (1250-1286)
- 3-Baron Robert DE ROS (1205-1269)
- +Lady Isabel D'AUBIGNY (1210-1248)
  - ○ 4-Sir Robert DE ROOS (1230-1274)
❖ **2-Countess Ada OF SCOTLAND (1165-1210)**
❖ **+Earl Patrick OF DUNBAR (1160-1232)**
- 3-Earl Patrick OF DUNBAR (1185-1248)
- +Countess Eupheme DE BRUS (1192-1267)
  - ○ 4-Lady Isabel OF DUNBAR (1220-1269)
+Queen Ermengard DE BEAUMONT (1174-1233)
❖ **2-King Alexander II OF SCOTLAND (1198-1249)**
❖ **+Queen Marie DE COUCY (1218-1285)**
- 3-King Alexander III OF SCOTLAND (1241-1286)
- +Queen Margaret PLANTAGENET (1240-1286)
  - ○ 4-Queen Margaret OF NORWAY (1261-1283)

Histories of some families not documented in the other books of this series.

The family histories of other early medieval aristocrats, including dukes, earls, counts, and famous knights, can be found on the website "Many Mini Biographies" identified at the beginning of this book.

Many from this time period can also be found in the books *Early European Aristocratic Families, Volumes I & II*, which are other books in this series.

Kings of Scotland

***

39979020. King William of Scotland & 39979021. Queen Ermengard de Beaumont & 19989907. Isabel Avenell

~1142, William born in Scotland, s/o 159916060. Henry of Scotland & 159916061. Ada de Warenne.

[--Earl William--]

6/12/1152, William made the Earl of Northumbria on the day his father was buried.

5/24/1153, Malcolm IV succeeded King David I of Scotland.

12/19/1154, Henry II crowned king of England.

~1157, Mistress 'Isabel' Avenel born in Scotland, d/o 39979814. Robert Avenell & 399798145. Eva ? ['Isabel' assumed from name of daughter.]

[--William--]

1157, William had to give up the Earl title to King Henry II.

6/24/1158, At the castle of Roxburgh, Malcolm, King of the Scots, to the bishops, abbots, earls, ... to Walter fitz Alan my steward ... Witnesses, ... William and David, the King's brothers, Earl Gospatrick, Earl Duncan, Richard de Moreville, ... Robert de Brus, ... (S) Charters and Doc's Relating to the Burgh of Paisley, 1902, P3.

1159, King Henry II, with the support of Malcolm IV of Scotland and William attending, attacked Toulouse, which Henry claimed by right of his wife. (S) Anglo-Norman Studies XII, 1989, P197.

1160, Robert de Quincy is recorded as a close companion of his cousin, future King William.

1160-62, William and his brother David, and their mother Ada, witnessed a charter of King Malcom to the abbey of Newbottle.

9/28/1162, Floris III, Count of Holland married Ada, sister of future King William the Lion of Scotland.

[--King William--]

12/24/1165, After the death of his brother Malcolm, age 24, William "the Lion", age 22, crowned King of Scotland. [The title "the Lion" came from the image on his standard.]

1166, King William the Lion of Scotland confirmed a grant of land made to the monks of Jedburgh by Margaret, mother of Henry [his father]. (S) History of the Berwickshire Naturalists' Club, 1887, P421.

3/1166, King William's passage to Normandy with King Henry II of England paid for by King Henry.

8/1166 at Mont St. Michael, France, King William sought an audience with King Henry II.

By 10/21/1166, King William started a return trip to Scotland.

1167 at Stirling, An agreement is formed between Durham Priory and Croyland Abbey (Lincs), in the presence of William, king of Scots.

1168, Malcolm MacEth, earl of Ross, died. During his reign King William did not regrant the earldom.

1168, King William concluded an alliance with France.

1169, Philip de Seton received a Charter from King William the Lion reaffirming the Lands of Seton, Winton and Wynchburgh. [One of the oldest Charters existant in Scotland.]

4/5/1170, William, King of the Scots, and his brother David present at the Council of Windsor of King II of England.

6/15/1170, at Westminster, King William does homage to the newly crowned [the day before] young King Henry of England.

6/10/1171, King William the Lion made a grant of Morgund to the earl of Marr. (S) Celtic Scotland, V3, 1880, P441.

4/1173, William attended the Easter court of King Louis VII in Paris [along with many other leaders.] William became a key rebel in the revolt of the sons of Henry II.

7/1173, Robert de Beaumont, earl of Leicester, Hugh de Keveloic, earl of Chester, King William of

Scotland, and Hugh le Bigod, earl of Norfolk, laid siege to Aumale, Meuf-marche, and Verneuil.

1173, William returned to Scotland.

1173, David sent to England by his brother King William of Scotland to aid the Earl of Leicester.

1/13/1174, Hugh, bishop of Durham, agrees on a truce with William, King of the Scots, until the close of Easter.

4/1174, William besieges Carlisle, held by Robert de Vaux.

7/11/1174, William ambushed and captured at the battle of Alnwick and imprisoned at Newcastle.

8/8/1174, From Portsmouth, King Henry took King William, his prisoner, to imprisonment in Falaise in Normandy.

9/30/1174, Through negotiations at Montlouis, King Henry II agreed to release all his prisoners except 4: the King of the Scots, the earl of Leicester, the earl of Chester [Hugh], and Ralph de Fougeres. (S) Henry II, Warren, 1973, P138.

[--Ermengard--]

~1174, Ermengard born in England, d/o 39979746. Richard de Beaumont.

10/11/1174, By the Treaty of Falaise, William agreed to submission to King Henry II and the paying of Henry's army occupying Scotland by taxing the Scots. By the treaty King Henry also got to pick William's bride.

12/8/1174, An agreement is formed between William, king of Scots, and Henry II, king of the English, son of the Empress Matilda. King William becomes the liege man of the king against all men, for Scotland, ... He also does homage and swears fealty to the King Henry, his son (i.e., Henry the young king), reserving the fealty due to his father the king. (S) POMS.

8/10/1175, at York castle, William, King of the Scots, his brother David, and the bishops, abbots, and nobles of Scotland attend court and do homage to King Henry II and his son Henry, the young king.

1/24/1176, King William attended the Great Council of King Henry II at Northampton, along with multiple Scottish bishops, and the archbishops of Canterbury and York.

10/1176 at Feckenham, Worcestershire, King William met King Henry II of England, bring to King Henry Gilbert fitz Fergus who had killed a relative of King William.

7/1/1177, King William, as leige of King Henry of England, attended King Henry's Great Council at Winchester under a summons to an army for Normandy [which expedition was postponed by intervention of the pope.]

10/14/1178, William founded the Abbey of Arbroath which was dedicated to Thomas à Becket.

1179, William and his brother David led a force northward into Easter Ross, establishing 2 castles.

3/30/1180 at Haddington, a dispute between Richard de Morville's family and the monks of Melrose [which became a famous controversy] required King William to gather a vast assemblage of the chief men of the Kingdom.

1180, King William recognized Gile Christ [Gilchrist] as earl of Mar.

1181, Pope Alexander excommunicated William the Lion of Scotland and put the kingdom under the interdict.

4/1181, King William travels to Normandy, landing at Barlfeur, to consult with King Henry about 2 bishops he had banished.

7/1181 at Gisors, King Henry II arbitrates a settlement between King Philip of France and the count of Flanders. William, King of the Scots was present.

7/26/1181, King William returns to England from Cherbourg with King Henry, landing at Portsmouth.

1181, While William was overseas Donald Meic Uilleim
(d.1187) of Inverness rebelled, taking control of
Ross.

11/22/1181, King William, under interdict, sent
Josecline, bishop of Glasgow, to Pope Lucius.

3/17/1182, Pope Lucius releases William of Scotland
from his interdict.

7/1182, Pope Lucius sent Rolland, archbishop elect of
Dol, with others as legates to negotiate between
King William and the rival bishops of St. Andrews.

1184, King Henry attempted to marry William to his
granddaughter Matilda, d/o Henry the Lion of
Saxony. [Refused by the Pope on grounds of
consanguinity.]

1184-85, King Henry decided on William's bride,
Ermengarde de Beaumont, granddaughter of Henry
I. Edinburgh castle was part of her dowery [which
King Henry now controlled], as well as land valued
at 140 marks annually and 40 knights' fees.

3/18/1185, At Clerkenwell [in London] a Great Council
decides that King Henry should not go on crusade.
William, King of the Scots, and his brother David,
both attended. King Henry restored the earldom of
Huntingdon to King William.

5/25/1186 at Oxford, King William attends the Great
Council of King Henry II, where it is arranged for
King William to marry the daughter of the Vicomte
of Beaumont. [King William was to have married
Matilda of Saxony, King Henry's granddaughter,
but consanguinity was an issue.]

1186, William competed in tournaments in northern
France.

7/1/1186, at Carlisle, King Henry sent King William
and his brother David to summon Roland fitz
Uctred to court.

[--William & Ermengarde--]

9/5/1186 at Woodstock, William married to
Ermengard, her father, Richard de Beaumont,
present at the wedding. [King Henry, by treaty of

Falaise, got to pick William's bride. Ermengarde's grandmother, 79959493. Constance fitz Roy, a natural d/o King Henry I (who had multiple 'recognized' children by mistresses).]

3/1187 at Crail, King William to Scone Abbey; he has granted the revenues in the queen's household which it already has in the king's, in the Spence and the kitchen, whenever the queen keeps her household separately.

1187, King William advanced with a large force into Inverness, supported by the Galwegians under Roland.

7/31/1187, King William defeated the rebelling Donald Bane at the battle of Muir of Mamgarvy on the Upper Spey. (S) DNB, V61, 1900, P334.

1/16/1188, Pope Clement III writes to Bishops ... recalling the great tribulations which the church of St Andrews ..., Clement commands that they should visit King William of Scotland, and warn him to desist from his rancour towards that bishop.

2/11/1188, King Henry imposes a tax of a 10th on moveable goods to be assessed in all of England to aid a crusade, and dispatches Hugh, bishop of Durham, to King William to press him to raise have the tax in Scotland. [King William refused to grant the tithe request.]

4/1189, King William gave the See of St. Andrews to his chancellor, Roger fitz Robert, earl of Leicester.

7/6/1189, Henry II of England died; Richard I succeeded.

12/5/1189 at Canterbury, Newly crowned King Richard I met with King William and agreed to the cancellation of William's Treaty of Falaise for a single payment of 10,000 silver marks which would help pay for his crusade. King Richard also returned all hostages to King William.

1189-90, King William to Earl David, his brother; has granted quittance of all teinds and customs which church of St Mary of Aberdeen and bishops of

Aberdeen used to have; in exchange for two measured ploughgates of land in Kennethmont.

Aft. 4/1/1190, King William has given the agreement (for a tack) made between Kelso Abbey.

1190 at Canterbury, King William did homage to King Richard. (S) Acts and Monuments of the Church, Foxe, 2004, P193.

1191, King William gave his daughter Isabel, widow of Robert de Brus, to Robert de Roos. (S) FMG.

3/13/1192, The Pope granted a Bull to King William that recognized the separate identity of the Scottish Church, and its independence of all ecclesiastical authorities apart from Rome.

2/2/1193, At Edinburgh in presence, and with agreement, of King William, Roger, bishop of St Andrews, to clergy of St Andrews diocese; he has established, and decreed agreement made between him and Prior Bertram and monks of Durham.

1193, William gave 2000 marks towards the ransom of King Richard I of England, who had been captured returning from the crusades. (S) Richard and John, Kings at War, McLynn, 2008, P233.

4/17/1194 at Winchester, William carried a ceremonial sword at King Richard's royal walk in Winchester after his return from captivity.

1194, William offered 15,000 marks to purchase Northumbria. King Richard did not want to give up his castles.

7/4/1195, King William to Kelso Abbey; has granted the donation and concession which Jocelin, bishop of Glasgow.

1195, William, lying ill at Clackmannan,and having no son, assembled his nobles and announced his appointed successor as Otho of Saxony, who would have to marry princess Margaret. (S) Royal Palaces of Scotland, Douglas-Irvine, 1911, P16.

1195-96, King William to David de la Haye, son of William de la Haye; has granted Errol.

6/16/1196, King William to Alexander, son of Philip of Seton; has granted the land which belonged to

Philip, his father, that is, Seton, Winton and Winchburgh.

1197-98, William the Lion reduced Harold, earl of Orkney, Caithness, and Shetland, who took arms at the instigation of his wife, sister of Donald Macheth. (S) The Cambridge Medieval History, V7, 1936, P560.

5/29/1198, King William grants that on the death of an abbot of Scone the canons of Scone may freely elect one of their convents to be abbot, with the counsel and consent of their king.

10/16/1198, King William to Walter, son of Walter Scott; has given Allardice for the service of one archer with a horse and haubergel and making common aid.

5/27/1199, John crowned king of England after the death of Richard I.

12/26/1199 at Forfar, King William to church of the Holy Trinity of bishopric of Moray and to Bishop Richard; has given teinds of his revenues of Moray and of his pleas throughout diocese of Moray and of his cain.

8/20/1200, King William to Hugh, son of Hugh of Benholm; has regiven Benholm.

10/30/1200, King John to William, king of Scots; he sends him Roger, bishop of St Andrews, Saher de Quincy, Hugh de Moreville and Richard de Maleville, by whom, and by these letters patent, he sends a safe conduct to William and his attendants.

11/1200, at Lincoln, William the Lion of Scotland did homage to King John. He obtained large grants and immunities. William's son-in-law, Baron Robert de Roos (9994952) escorted him from Scotland.

1201-02, King William to Inchaffray Abbey; has granted the donation which Earl Gilbert of Strathearn made.

2/1202, King William again visited with the King of England at Yorkshire. (S) DNB, Watkins, 1899, P376.

3/1202-7/1202, An agreement was made to settle the dispute between Bishop Roger and St Andrews Cathedral Priory sealed by King William.

1203, William was ill and housed at Traquair.

11/4/1203, King William to Holyrood Abbey; has granted donation which William de Vieuxpont made of land of Ogilface.

5/9/1204 at Selkirk, King William announces that in dispute between Kelso and Melrose about marches between Melrose and Bowden, he held a hearing at Melrose ..., judgement in favor of Kelso Abbey.

1205, King William by charter founded Ayr as a royal burgh.

7/24/1205, King John writes to the king of Scots [William], informing him that his messengers are to be retained ..., due to the death of H[ubert], archbishop of Canterbury. As he is awaiting a response, he sends R[oger], constable of Chester ... so that William can deal with the relevant business. John is pleased by the exception regarding the land of Tynedale, as contained in William's letters.

1206, Earl William Longespee escorted King William the Lion of Scotland to visit King John at York. [While there, William is recorded as having cured a case of Scrofula by touching and blessing a child with the ailment.]

6/6/1207, Pope Innocent III writes to the bishop of Brechin, the abbot of Scone and the prior of Arbroath, ... chapter of St Andrews ... the Noble Man, S[aher] de Quincy had usurped the patronage of the church by violence, ..., wishes to litigate the case before the king [William], he compelled the chapter to appear before the king so that the case could be examined.

1207, Walter, a royal chaplain, [supposedly] obtained the position of bishop of Glasgow partly by bribing Queen Ermengard.

2/29/1208 at Forfar, King William to Dunfermline Abbey; has granted donation which Robert of London, his son, made of Outh.

11/6/1208 at Selkirk, King William has granted settlement in his presence and in his full court of dispute between Patrick, earl of Dunbar, and Melrose Abbey anent pasture on west bank of Leader Water; settlement is made with consent of Earl Patrick's son and heir, Patrick.

7/1209, King John, with 800 knights, 45 of them household knights, made a short-lived invasion into Scotland. (S) English Historical Review, V110, 1995, P284. [William ended the incursion promising money and the marriage of his eldest daughters to English barons.]

4/10/1209, King John writes to W[illiam], king of Scots, expressing joy at his recovery, and comes to meet him ... He sends as an escort R[anulf], earl of Chester, W., earl of Ferrers, P. [...], [Robert fitz] Roger, R[oger], constable of Chester, Robert de Ros and Eustace de Vescy. The king desires to confer with him and settle matters long discussed between them.

8/4/1209, Llywelyn ap Iorwerth commanded his forces in support of King John at the battle of Norham against King William of Scotland [who lost the battle]. (S) Land of My Fathers, Evans, 1993, P211.

8/7/1209, King William binds himself to pay to his lord, King John of England, in 4 equal instalments of 3,750 marks each, the sum of 15,000 marks, ...; in order to observe agreements made between himself and King John as established in charters issued by both parties. To ensure payment, he has given to King John the keeping of hostages he already has, ..., except for his two daughters whom he has now released to King John. Queen Ermengard acted as a mediator in the negotiations.

1/7/1210 at Stirling, King William to the church of St Cuthbert of Kirkcudbright; has granted donation which Alan, son of Roland the constable, made of that part of Sypland.

1/1211, King William sent the earl of Atholl, the earl of Mar, Malcom, son of Morgrund, and Thomas

Durward [each representing families claiming Mar] with 4,000 men to suppress a rebellion in Ross and Moray. (S) Medieval Scotland, Barrow, 1998, P175.

6/27/1211 at Edinburgh, Charter by King William granting his firm peace to all attending the fair at Glasgow. (S) Charters ... City of Glasgow, V1, Pt2, P430.

10/2/1211 at Forres, King William to William Comyn has granted right to have a burgh at Kirkintilloch, and market every Thursday with liberties and rights pertaining to burghs.

1211-12, William the Lion's campaign against the MacWilliam rebels.

2/1212, Queen Ermengard acted as a negotiator when King William and King John met at Durham; resulting in a peace agreement, part of which stipulated that Prince Alexander would be given an English wife.

5/31/1212 at Edinburgh, The case called between Abbot P[atrick] and the convent of Dunfermline and Philip de Mowbray and his wife, Galiena, concerning the church of Inverkeithing before papal judges ..., the suit was settled thus. In the presence of Lady Ermengarde, queen of Scots ...

7/1/1212 at Edinburgh, Philip de Moubray and Galiena, his wife, for the welfare of their lord William, king of Scotland, and of Sir Alexander his son, have granted and by this their present charter established, and in the presence of Lady Ermengarde, queen of Scotland, and of Sir William, bishop of St Andrews, quitclaimed in perpetuity to Dunfermline Abbey, all the teinds of grain pertaining to the church of Inverkeithing.

2/25/1213 at Selkirk, King William to Arbroath Abbey; has given, granted, and established various possessions.

10/28/1213, Pope Innocent III commands William, king of Scotland, and Alexander his son, now that peace is made between John, king of England, and the priesthood in England, to remain in fealty to the king and his heirs.

12/7/1213 at Edinburgh, King William has granted convention made at Edinburgh in his full court between Maurice, elder, of Menteith, and Maurice, younger, his brother, of earldom of Menteith, which Maurice, younger, had claimed as his right and heritage and which Maurice, elder, resigned into king's hand, and king delivered to Maurice, younger, as his right.

11/25/1214, Fulk de Sulis witnessed a grant of Meikleour and Lethendy by King William to Gilbert, earl of Strathearn. (S) POMS.

10/27/1214, Pope Innocent III writes to the bishops of St Andrews and Aberdeen … he wishes to remind and advise the king of Scotland [William] to defend the church of Glasgow and other churches in his realm.

12/4/1214, William died, his reign the 2nd longest in Scotish history. He was an effective monarch. New burghs founded, criminal law clarified, the responsibilities of justices and sheriffs widened, and trade expanded.

[--Ermengard--]

12/1214, Ermengard stayed with the body of her husband while her son was taken to Scone for his coronation.

3/4/1215, Ermengarde buried William at Aberbrothock where she mourned for 14 days.

10/28/1216, Henry III, age 9, crowned king of England.

12/7/1219, Pope Honorius III commands Pandulph, bishop-elect of Norwich, papal legate, to enquire and report to the pope touching information laid against the bishop of Glasgow … he gave 100 marks to Philip de Valognes, the king's chamberlain, and promised a much larger sum to the queen [Ermengard] to procure his appointment to the see by the king.

6/18/1221, King Alexander II for Joan, eldest sister of Sir Henry, king of England, his spouse; has granted in dower £1,000 of land, … should the queen his mother (Ermengarde) survive the king and be unwilling to confer her lands of Kinghorn and Crail on Joan in dower, the deficiency is to be met by king's heirs in castles and castleries.

10/12/1225, An agreement is formed between Queen Ermengarde, mother of the lord King Alexander (II), and Sir Adam of Stawell, over 1000 marks which the lady queen owed Adam of Stawell for the quitclaim.

Aft. 6/24/1226, Adam of Stawell has received at London in the Temple of London 1000 marks from Lady Ermengarde, Queen of Scots, mother of the lord king of Scotland, in the presence of brothers Simon and Morica, chaplains of the Temple, and other brothers of the same Temple, for the lands Balmerino.

Bef. 1229, Ermengarde devoted herself to founding a Cistercian abbey at Balmerino in Fife; and oversaw the construction.

12/13/1229, Monks from Melros settled at the Cistercian abbey. Ermengard and her son were frequent visitors.

2/11/1233, Ermengard died; buried before the high alter at Balmerino.

(S) Scotland's Historic Heraldry, McAndrew, 2006. (S) The Wars of Scotland, Brown, 2004. (S) Scottish Queens, Marshall, 2004, P18. (S) From Domesday Book to Magna Carta, Poole, 1955, P279. (S) Court, Household, and Itinerary of King Henry II, Eyton, 1878. (S) People of Medieval Scotland.

Children of William and ?:
* ❖ **Ada of Scotland (973530389), born ~1165 in Scotland.**

Child of William and Mistress 'Isabel':
* **Isabel of Scotland (9994953), born ~1175 in England. [Natural daughter]**

Children of William and Ermengarde:
* **Margaret of Scotland, born bef. 1195 in Scotland.**
1219, Margaret betrothed to Thibaut IV, comte de Champagne [not finalized.]
1221, Margaret married Hubert de Burgh, earl of Kent.
1227, Hubert created earl of Kent.
1232, Hubert divorced Margaret.
1259, Margaret died, buried at Black Friars, London.

* **King Alexander II of Scotland (19989510), born 8/24/1198 at Haddington, Lothian, Scotland.**

* **Majorie of Scotland, born ? in Scotland.**
8/1/1235, Majorie married Gilbert Marshall, earl of Pembroke. (S) FMG. [Majorie's dowery, 10000 marks.]
6/27/1241, Gilbert died after falling from his horse in a tournament.
11/17/1244, Majorie died, buried in the Church of Preaching Friars, London.

***
19989510. King Alexander II of Scotland

8/24/1198, Alexander II of Scotland, born at Haddington, Lothian, Scotland, s/o 39979020. King William of Scotland & 39979021. Ermengard de Beaumont.

Bef. 3/17/1199, Alexander named in an agreement between Sir Roger, bishop of St Andrews, and Abbot Henry and the convent of Arbroath.

1200, Alexander betrothed to Marie, d/o King Philip of France [not finalized.]

10/12/1201 at Musselburgh, the Scottish nobility swore fealty to Alexander II.

2/1212, Alexander's mother Queen Ermengard acted as a negotiator when King William and King John of England met at Durham; resulting in a peace agreement, part of which stipulated that Prince Alexander would be given an English wife.

[--Alexander Knighted--]

3/8/1212 at London, King John of England knighted Alexander at Clerkenwell priory.

10/28/1213, Pope Innocent III commands William, king of Scotland, and Alexander his son, now that peace is made between John, king of England, and the priesthood in England, to remain in fealty to the king and his heirs.

12/6/1213 at Edinburgh, Alexander put his seal on an agreement between Muiredach (Mauricius) earl of Menteith and Muiredach his younger brother, due to a lawsuit that was between them over the earldom of Menteith, which Muiredach junior sought as his right and his inheritance.

12/4/1214, Alexander's father died.

[--King Alexander--]

12/5/1214 at Scone, Alexander crowned King of the Scots, "with more pomp and ceremony than anyone before him." All seven Scottish earls were present.

1214, Richard de Montealto, justiciary of Scotland, witnessed a confirmation of King Alexander II.

1215, The barons of northern England renewed their homage to King Alexander for his English lands.

1215, Alexander's forces defeated a revolt of the cals of Meic Uilleim and MacHeths.

1215, Alexander led forces in northern England as the barons revolted against King John. Alexander's brother-in-law, Eustace de Vesci, lord of Alnwick in Northumberland, was a leading baron in the revolt.

[--Magna Carta--]

6/1215, The signing of the Magna Carta by King John included a promise to answer grievances of Alexander's vassals. [King John then arranged for all of the barons to be excommunicated – starting a war.]

7/7/1215 at Kelso, King Alexander II to John, king of England; informs him that he has appointed William, bishop of St Andrews, Philip de Mowbray, Robert de St Germain, Walter Lindsey, Ingram de Balliol, and John Maxwell with full authority to negotiate concerning business he has against John to be transacted in John's court.

10/22/1215 at Felton, The rebel barons of Northumberland gave homage to Alexander as their rightful lord. Alexander attacked Norham with little success.

1/1216, King John led a successful counterattack against Alexander and the northern barons, burning 4 Scottish burghs and capturing Carlisle.

9/1216 at Dover, England, Alexander paid homage to invading Prince Louis of France for three shires in northern England. Alexander conquered Cumberland and followed with incursions into Northumberland estates of English-supporting barons.

10/28/1216, Henry III, age 9, crowned king of England.

1/16/1217, Pope Honorius III writes to King Alexander II ... The pope earnestly commands and urges him ..., that having regard to the tender age of ..., Henry the king of England, ..., he returned to the fealty of the said king, and his devotion to the apostolic see, notwithstanding his disloyal oaths made to Louis, the Dauphin (heir to the crown of France).

5/1217, The loyal forces of England defeated the English rebel barons, who were supported by the French, at the battle of Lincoln.

9/12/1217, Prince Louis and Alexander signed the Treaty of Kingston-Lambeth with the English. [Which was rejected by Prince Llywelyn ap Iorwerth (19989730) of Gwynedd in Wales.]

[--Marie--]

~1218, Marie, a great-great granddaughter of King Louis VI of France, born in Picardy, France, d/o §§Lord Enguerrand III of Coucy (d.1242) & Marie de Montmirel (b.1192, d.1267). [According to chronicler Matthew Paris (d.1259), Marie was beautiful and very wealthy.]

11/21/1218, Pope Honorius III grants to Alexander, king of Scots, and his successors, following the example of his predecessors Popes Celestine and Innocent and considering that the Scottish church, in which there are the following dioceses, St Andrews, Dunblane, Glasgow, Dunkeld, Brechin, Aberdeen, Moray, Ross and Caithness, was subject immediately to the apostolic see, that no one except the pope or his legate shall promulgate a sentence of interdict or excommunication.

1219, Because the restoration of lands between England and Scotland was not progressing, the papal Legate Randulph was assigned to negotiate a settlement.

10/3/1219 at Edinburgh, King Alexander II for Coupar Angus Abbey; with agreement of bishop of St Andrews, has given them the church of Airlie.

[--Alexander & Joan--]

6/15/1220, King Alexander II makes known that he undertakes to marry Joan, eldest sister of Sir Henry, king of England, ... and, if not, he swears that he will marry Isabel, younger sister of King Henry, within fifteen ... signatories include the earl of Buchan (William Comyn), Alan of Galloway, constable, and other barons of the king, that is, Philip de Mowbray, Walter Olifant, Duncan of Carrick, Henry de Balliol, Thomas Durward, John of Maxwell, David Marshal, Walter Comyn ...

8/2/1220 at York, A final settlement on the issue of lands between England and Scotland was signed between King Alexander and King Henry's representative, Stephen de Segrave, knight.

1221, Alexander fought a naval engagement at Argyll against a Galwegian (Irish) fleet led by Somerled, son of Gillecolum.

12/25/1221, King Henry III knighted Alexander and 20 of his nobles in the cathedral at York. (S) Historical and Scientific Survey of York, 1906, P45.

[--Alexander & Joanna--]

12/26/1221 at York, Alexander 1st married Joanna, age 11, eldest daughter of King John of England. [No children.]

2/6/1222, "A. King of Scots" has made fine with the king [Henry III] by £200 for having custody of the heirs of David de Lindes', with their marriage, and with all lands that fall to the heirs by inheritance of the lands formerly of John de Limes', their kinsman. (S) FRsHIII.

1222, Alexander marched north with an army after the murder of Adam, bishop of Caithness. Earl John of Orkeny was forced to surrender the murderers and had his lands taken, which were restored the next year.

5/9/1223 at Ayr, King Alexander II has granted, and by his charter established, to his burgh and burgesses of Ayr all liberties and customs which his other burghs and burgesses have.

1223, Richard, son of King John, with King Alexander II of Scotland – his brother-in-law, made a pilgrimage to Canterbury.

1224, King Alexander imposed a tax of £10,000 as a subsidy for the marriage of his sisters.

7/5/1224 at Musselburgh, King Alexander II writes to Gilbert, bishop of Caithness, the abbot of Kinloss, and Henry, dean of Ross, noting that he desires to transfer the See of Moray to a site beside Elgin.

5/9/1225 at Glasgow, King Alexander II for Glasgow Cathedral; has granted donation which Robert of London, his brother, made for its lighting of one stone of wax, to be received yearly from Roger de Sancta Fide and Robert of Newham and their heirs.

10/27/1225, By a fine that the king's [Henry III] faithful and beloved brother Alexander, King of Scots, has made with the king, he has granted to the same king, until the full age of the heirs of H. Bigod, formerly earl of Norfolk, those 50 librates of land. (S) FRsHIII.

11/22/1225, Charter by King Alexander II confirming to Bishop Walters and his successors the right to have a Burgh at Glasgow. (S) Charters ... City of Glasgow, V1, Pt2, P430.

1225-28, Roger le Bigod, a ward of his brother-in-law Alexander II of Scotland. [Roger married Alexander's sister Isabella.]

3/11/1226, King Alexander grants to burgh, burgesses, and inhabitants of Dumbarton an annual fair of eight days duration with all customs and liberties of fairs of burghs of Roxburgh and Haddington.

2/26/1227 at Linlithgow, King Alexander II has built a burgh at Dingwall in Ross and to burgh and his burgesses there he has granted all liberties and free customs enjoyed by his burgesses of Inverness.

8/15/1227, There is a dispute between the [Alexander] King of Scots and R. earl of Chester. (S) FRsHIII.

4/22/1228, Inspeximus ... charter of Roger le Bigod, son of Hugh le Bigod, ... bound to lodge £1,000 of silver at the New Temple on behalf of Alexander, king of Scots, and to hold the said king harmless, who was bound to deposit that sum there ... 500 marks which the said king has given to Isabel, wife of the said Roger, ... (S) CChRs.

6/30/1228 at Elgin, King Alexander II has given land of 'Robynfeld', by its right marches, to maintain bridge of Spey.

1228, Alexander traveled to Moray after the death of Thomas of Thirlestane; and began eliminating the MacWilliams, executing all of the klan, including a baby girl. This started the rise of the Comyns. William Comyn, justiciar of Scotia and warden of Moray, had captured the MacWilliams leaders. [Alexander's father had also had to handle revolts of this clan.]

3/10/1229 at Edinburgh, King Alexander II for Margaret, his younger sister; has given, for her marriage, all his land of Tynedale, to be held for one hawk yearly at feast of St Michael, reserving to king the homages and services of William Comyn and William de Ros, and advowson of the church of Simonburn.

12/1229, Alexander and King Henry III kept their Christmas feast together at York.

1230, Alexander made Walter Comyn lord of Badenoch, a large fife stretching from Lochaber to the upper valley of Spey.

1230, A Norse fleet sailed into Clyde, landed on Bute, and stormed Alan of Galloway's castle of Rothesay. King Alexander led an army in relief.

7/10/1230, King Alexander II for Dryburgh Abbey; has granted all donations, possessions and liberties which were granted and established to them from time of King David, his great-grandfather, and King

Malcolm, his uncle, and Sir William, the king, his father. (S) POMS.

2/3/1231, King Alexander II announces that he has founded an abbey of Cistercian order at Balmerino in Fife.

4/27/1231, Pope Gregory IX writes ... As the pope loves the English king, as a special son of the Apostolic See, and embraces Alexander as devoted to the Roman Church, and thus earnestly desires to see them in the bond of unity, and discord between them grieves and distracts him, he thinks it fitting to ask and exhort the king of Scots to study to observe more fully his obligations to Henry, ...

1231, King Alexander made Walter, son of Alan of Galloway, Grand Justiciary of Scotland, replacing Walter Comyn.

9/6/1231 at Linlighgow, King Alexander II for Absalon, son of Macbeth; has granted donation which Maldoven, earl of Lennox, made of island called Clairinsh (STL), with license of common fishing in king's stank in Loch Lomond.

2/10/1232 at Selkirk, King Alexander II to his sheriffs; command to prosecute cases of monks of Balmerino Abbey against malefactors just as his own and takes monks and their men under his protection.

2/7/1233, King Alexander II for Holyrood Abbey; has granted donation which Roger de Quincy made of teinds of his hay of Tranent.

10/12/1233, King Alexander II, for Arbroath Abbey; at petition of Alan Durward, has granted wood of Trustach, which Alan's father, Thomas Durward, had granted to monks, in free forest. No one may fell timber or hunt there without their license, on pain of king's full forfeiture of £10.

7/18/1234, Charter of donation of King Alexander II to monks of Coupar Angus of £10 which king used to receive each year from abbot of Coupar Angus for land of Glenisla.

1/13/1235, Pope Gregory IX commands the bishop of
Moray ..., duplicate letters of credit were given ... a
debt of 1,060 marks, which, when the king paid,
the clerk kept the duplicate letters, refusing to give
them up. The pope orders that, if any further debt
is contracted at any time by means of the letters
withheld, the king [Alexander] is not to be
molested in regard to it.

7/1235, Alexander led an army to suppress a revolt in
Galloway. Early in the campaign, Alexander's forces
were ambushed. Alexander was saved by the
arrival of forces under Ferchar, earl of Ross. The
next day a peace was arranged.

10/13/1235, Charter by King Alexander II granting to
Bishop William of Glasgow his chancellor ... should
be exempted from paying toll through his whole
kingdom, ... (S) Charters ... City of Glasgow, V1,
Pt2, P431.

7/23/1236, King Alexander II for Richard of Moray;
has handed over at feu-ferme Meikle Kincorth ...
Witnesses ... Alan Durward.

12/27/1236 at Stirling, King Alexander II for
Dunfermline Abbey; in exchange for alms monks
used to receive from his demesnes at Kinghorn and
Crail in wheat, flour, oats, malt, meal and money,
and for all their rights in kitchens of king and
queen, has given his land of Dollar in feu of
Clackmannan.

5/7/1237, Cardinal Legate Otho was sent from Rome
to restore peace between Scotland and England.
(S) Ecclesiastical Chronicle for Scotland, V1,
Gordon, 1875, P152.

6/1237, Alexander's cousin and potential successor,
John of Scotland, earl of Huntingdon, died.

9/25/1237 at York, By treaty, Alexander II of Scotland
asserted to King Henry of England that he was
owed Northumberland as dowry of Joanna. King
Henry acknowledged a grant of Tynedale in
Northumberland, as well as the Earldom of Chester.

3/4/1238, Joan died in Essex, buried at Tarant
Crawford Abbey, co. Dorset.

[--Alexander--]

7/28/1238, King Alexander II for Maldoven, son of
Alwin, earl of Lennox; he has given earldom of
Lennox, which his father held, except castle of
Dumbarton and land of Murroch.
2/23/1239, King Alexander II for Newbattle Abbey; he
has granted donation David Lindsay made of land
of Glengonnar and Glencaple in territory of
Crawford.

[--Alexander & Marie--]

5/15/1239 in Roxburgh, Alexander married Marie de
Coucy. [Marie brought with her a large retinue of
French supporters.]
4/30/1240 at Elgin, Andrew, bishop of Moray, ...
announce those things which prior and convent of
Pluscarden have from grants ... of Alexander, king
of Scots, which they have caused to be read
publicly in synod to avoid confusion.
8/1/1240 at Stirling, King Alexander II for Gillascop
MacGilcrist; has given 5 pennylands of Finchairn ...
8/28/1241 at Selkirk, King Alexander II to John de
Vaux, sheriff of Edinburgh, Gilbert Fraser, sheriff of
Traquair, ... command to go in person to Leithen ...
to cause an extent to be made ..., of pasture of
Leithen Hopes.
10/31/1241, Alexander II, King of the Scots to the
Provosts of Perth, greetings. ... (S) Ancient Capital
of Scotland, V2, Cowan, 1904, P387.
7/15/1242 at Scone, King Alexander II to his sheriff
and bailies of Traquair; command to imprison all in
their bailliary whom bishop of Glasgow, his
archdeacon, official or dean shall present to them
as having remained under sentence of
excommunication for forty days, until
excommunicates reconcile themselves to the
Church.

912/1242 at Kirkton, King Alexander II for William, bishop of Glasgow, and his successors; he has granted that they may hold in free forest their lands around Glasgow.

1243, King Alexander made a charter and donation to the monks of Newbottle. (S) Scottish Notes and Queries, V11, Bulloch, 1898, P83.

6/9/1243 at Edinburgh, King Alexander II for Glasgow Cathedral; has granted donation John de Vaux made of 5 marks yearly.

7/1244, Alexander II of Scotland [King Henry's brother-in-law and widower of Joanna] invaded north England.

1244, Alexander began efforts to buy the Western Isles from the king of Norway.

8/1244, King Henry, at Newcastle, negotiated a peace that involved the future marriage of their children, and gave Alexander custody of the disputed lands in Cumberland.

12/1244 at Newcastle, Concession and promise to keep the peace sent by Alexander II to King Henry III by the prior of Tynemouth. Witnesses: ... Alan Durward, ... Patrick, earl of Dunbar, ... Alexander Comyn, earl of Buchan, ... Roger de Mowbray, ... "our sworn man" Nicholas Soulis, lord of Liddesdale, ...

5/5/1245, Pope Innocent IV grants the King of Scotland [Alexander] to be free from the greater excommunication if by chance he or his household should have dealings with those excommunicated for disobedience to ecclesiastical judges. The same to the Queen of Scotland; The same to Alexander, the king's son.

7/27/1245, Pope Innocent IV, at the request of the king of Scotland, writes to the bishops of St Andrews, Dunkeld and Dunblane, that since the body of Margaret, queen of Scotland, of bright memory, may emit boundless miracles, he had her included in a list of saints. He thus commands them to examine diligently her life, merits, and miracles and what they find they may narrate it to the pope in writing, under their seals, through a messenger.

11/12/1246, King Alexander II for Scone Abbey; has granted grants which Roger de Quincy, earl of Winchester, made.

2/8/1247, King Alexander II for Melrose Abbey; has given fishery on River Tweed which is called fishery of Selkirk.

1247, The Galwegians revolted. Faced with a siege and little chance of relief, Roger le Bigod and a few men fought their way out and rode off to seek help from King Alexander II of Scotland, who raised forces to suppress the rebellion. (S) DNB, 1885, P263.

3/14/1248, Pope Innocent IV indulges to the king of Scotland, by advice of his confessor and physicians, to eat eggs, butter, cheese, and fresh meat, during Lent.

11/20/1248, Nicholao de Sules, lord of Liddesdale, and sheriff of Roxburgh, accused by King Henry III of England and King Alexander II of Scotland of particular injury against the March laws and customs.

12/4/1248, Nicholas de Soulis witnessed a charter of King Alexander II at Edinburgh.

1/13/1249, King Alexander II for abbot and convent of Dunfermline; has granted that they may hold in free warren their feu of Musselburgh.

1249, Alexander led an army west to force submission of Ewen of Lorn, Lord of Argyll. Alexander raised a fleet to carry the war into the Isles.

7/8/1249, King Alexander II for mensa of bishopric of Argyll; has given church of St Bridget (of Kilbride) in Lorn.

7/8/1249, Alexander died of illness on the island of Kerrera; buried in Melrose Abbey, Roxburghshire; his son Alexander succeeding.

[--Marie--]

8/6/1249, Queen Marie had eight-year-old Alexander III crowned at Scone. [Marie, a foreigner, was not selected as the regent of Alexander.]

6/9/1250 at Dunfermline, Marie and Alexander present for the canonization of Saint Margaret of Scotland.

1250, Marie moved back to Picardy, France, but often travelled back to Scotland. [In France she met her next husband.]

[--Marie & Jean--]

1257, Marie married 2nd Jean de Brienne, Grand Butler of France [his 2nd, no children].

1260-62, Marie and Jean members of the royal council of Scotland.

1262, Alexander III attained majority. Marie returned to France with Jean.

1268, Jean de Brienne died.

[--Marie--]

2/1275, After the death of her daughter-in-law Margaret a year earlier, Marie arranged a new marriage between Alexander and Yolande of Dreux.

1276, Marie made a pilgrimage to the shrine of St. Thomas Becket in Canterbury.

7/1285, Marie died, buried in a tomb constructed at Newbattle Abbey, Scotland.

(S) The Historians of Scotland, 1880. (S) People of Medieval Scotland. (S) The Wars of Scotland, Brown, 2004. (S) Reign of Alexander II, Oram, 2005.

Child of Alexander and a mistress:
- ❖ **Margery of Scotland (9994755), born ~1220 in Scotland.**

Child of Alexander and Marie:
- ❖ **King Alexander III, born 9/4/1241 in Scotland.**

***

King Alexander III of Scotland

9/4/1241, Alexander III born in Scotland, s/o King Alexander II of Scotland & Queen Marie de Coucy.

7/8/1249, Alexander's father died, Alexander III succeeding.

[--King Alexander--]

8/6/1249, Queen Marie had almost eight-year-old Alexander III crowned at Scone.

[--Alexander III & Margaret--]

12/26/1251, Alexander married to Margaret, d/o King Henry III of England. [At the ceremony King Henry demanded Alexander perform homage for Scotland, but the regents did not comply.]

9/20/1252 at Roxburgh castle, King Henry III of England dissolved the regents governing Scotland and named himself "principal counselor to the King of Scotland" [for the years until Alexander was of age.] Many Scots refused to sign the ordinance, but it was signed by Alexander (age 11).

9/20/1255, Announcement of change in Scottish council by King Alexander III to King Henry III; ... Witnessed: ... [4 bishops, 4 abbots] ... [8 earls] ... Alan Durward ... Roger de Mowbray ... John de Vaux ... Alexander Comyn, earl of Buchan, ... Robert of Roos, ... Nicholas Soulis, ... Margaret, daughter of Henry III, queen of Scots. [This was a major shift in power in Scotland in favor of Alan Durward, Justiciar of Scotland.]

1257, The losing party in the power shift, the Comyn family, seized Alexander and forced the regency to consist of a member from both groups.

9/4/1262, Alexander III attained majority. Queen Marie returned to France with her second husband Jean.

1262, Alexander announced his intention to continue efforts against the Western Isles (Orkney islands), the effort of his father at the time of his death.

Alexander made a formal claim to the Norwegian king Haakon.

1263, King Haakon invaded Scotland at the Isle of Arran, the largest island in the lower Firth of Clyde. King Alexander delayed negotiations knowing that the stormy season was approaching, which eventually led to damage to Haakon's fleet.

10/1263, Haakon attacked. The sea Battle of Largs, on the Firth of Clyde, was indecisive.

12/15/1263, King Haakon died in the Western Isles.

11/24/1265, Alexander became the ruler of the Isle of Man on the death of King Magnus Olafsson.

7/2/1267, The Treaty of Perth between Magnus IV and Alexander III ceded the Isle of Man and the Western Isles to Scotland in return for money.

2/27/1274, Margaret died at Cupar castle, Fife, Scotland; buried at Dunfermline.

[--Alexander--]

2/1275, After the death of her daughter-in-law Margaret a year earlier, Queen Marie arranged a new marriage between Alexander and Yolande of Dreux.

7/1285, Alexander's mother Queen Marie died.

[--Alexander III & Yolande--]

10/14/1285 at Jedburgh abbey, Alexander married Yolande de Dreux, d/o Count Robert IV & Beatrice of Montfort.

3/19/1286, Alexander died after suffering injuries from falling from a horse. Yolande was pregnant at the time. The child died soon after birth.

[--Yolande--]

Yolande married 2nd Arthur, duke of Brittany, whose mother was Beatrice, d/o King Henry III.

Children of Alexander and Margaret:
* **Margaret of Scotland, born 2/28/1261 in Scotland.**

99

8/1281 in Bergen on the west coast of Norway,
Margaret married King Eric II of Norway.
4/9/1283, Queen Margaret died after giving berth to
her only child.

❖ **Margaret of Scotland, born 2/28/1261 in Scotland.**
1281 in Bergen on the west coast of Norway, Margaret
married King Eric II of Norway.
Child:
   • **Margaret of Norway**, born 4/1283 in Norway,
   and known as the "Maid of Norway."
9/1290 Margaret, the only surviving descendent of
deceased King Alexander III of Scotland, died at
St Margaret's Hope in Orkney. This began a
succession struggle between 13 competitors.

❖ **Prince Alexander of Scotland, born 1/21/1264 in Scotland.**
1/17/1284, Alexander, age 19, died at Lindores, Fife,
Fifeshire, Scotland.

Kings of Hungary

***

189110360. King Geza II of Hungary & 189110361. Queen Euphrosyne of Kiev

[--Grandfather Almos & Father Bela--]

~1105, Bela born in Hungary, s/o §§Duke Almos of Hungary (b.~1080).

1112-15, [Geza's father] Bela, and [Geza's grandfather] Duke Almos, blinded on the order of Almos' brother, King Coloman of Hungary. [Almos had been trying to overthrow Coloman.] Almos and Bela were put in the monastery of Domos.

1116, Stephen II, s/o Coloman, succeeded as King of Hungary.

1125, Almos fled the monastery to Constantinople.

9/1127, Almos died in Constantinople.

[--Bela & Helena--]

By 1129, Stephen II, having no heirs, and joyous on learning that Bela was alive, arranged for his marriage to Helena, giving them Tolna.

[--Geza--]

1130, Geza born in Tolna, Hungary, eldest s/o §§King Béla II 'the Blind' of Hungary & Queen Helena of Rascia. [Rascia near Kosovo, Russia.]

[--Euphrosyne--]

~1130, Euphrosyne born in Kiev, d/o §§Grand Prince Mstislav Vladimirovich of Novgorod & Princess Cristina Ingesdotter of Sweden.

[--King Bela--]

4/1131, Geza's father Bela succeeded his cousin, King Stephen II.

1131, Queen Helena took Géza and his younger brother, Ladislaus, to an assembly held at Arad, where she ordered the massacre of 68 noblemen by whose counsel Bela had been blinded.

1132, Boris, s/o King Coloman's 2nd wife who had been repudiated for adultery, invaded Hungary from Poland.

7/22/1132, Bela's forces allied with Austrians defeated Boris at a battle on the river Sajó.

1133, 1134, 1137, and 1139, Bela was visited by his ally Soběslav I of Bohemia.

6/1139, Bela arranged the engagement of his daughter Sophia with Henry, son of the new German king Conrad III.

2/13/1141, Bela 'the blind' died, buried in the Székesfehérvár Cathedral. Geza succeeded his father Bela, his mother, and her brother Belos acting as guardians.

[--King Geza--]
2/16/1141, Geza crowned King.

1141, Geza, 'By the Grace of God, King of Hungary, Dalmatia, Croatia and Rama' signed a charter confirming the privileges of the citizens of Split in Dalmatia.

1145, Boris Kalamanos, a pretender to the crown of Hungary, led German mercenaries into Hungary and captured the fortress of Pressburg.

1146, Geza, of age, invaded Austria in retaliation for previous incursions into his lands.

1146, Euphrosyne's father died, her brother Iziaslav succeeding.

[--Geza & Euphrosyne--]
8/1146, Geza married Euphrosyne.

9/11/1146, Geza won the Battle of the Fischa on the border between Hungary and Austria.

6/1147, German crusaders marched through Hungary on their way to the Holy Land.

8/1147, French crusaders journeyed through Hungary.

1148-1155, Geza supported Iziaslav II of Kiev [Geza's brother-in-law] in Kiev-local conflicts.

1154, Géza invaded the Byzantine Empire and laid siege to Braničevo.

10/1154, Pope Anastasius IV declared Géza's rule in Dalmatia unlawful.

1158-60, Géza supported Frederick I, Holy Roman Emperor, against the Lombard League. [Italians that supported the Pope against German domination of the papal states.]

1/1158, Géza accepted Emperor Frederick Barbarossa as arbitrator in his conflict with his younger brother Stephen.

9/1/1159, Pope Adrian IV died. The Cardinals split and two Popes were elected [The second called the Anti-Pope.]

1161, Geza changed allegiance from Pope Victor IV to Pope Alexander III, promising the Pope to not depose or transfer prelates with his consent.

By 1162, Geza organized a separate appanage duchy, containing Dalmatia, Croatia and other territories, for his younger son, Béla.

5/31/1162, Geza died, his son Stephen succeeding.

Family notes:

Abū Hāmid stated that every country feared Géza's attack, because of the many armies he has at his disposal and his great courage, also observing that Geza employed Muslim soldiers. (S) The Travels of Abū Hāmid al-Andalusī al-Gharnātī, 1130-55, P.82-3.

Children of Geza and Euphrosyne:

❖ **Stephen of Hungary, born ? in Hungary.**

1172, Stephen died; his brother succeeding.

❖ **Bela III of Hungary (94555180) born ~1150 in Hungary.**

❖ **Elizabeth of Hungary, born ? in Hungary.**

1157, Elizabeth married to Frederick of Bohemia.

❖ **Odola of Hungary, born ? in Hungary.**
Odala married to Sviatopluk of Bohemia.

❖ **Helena of Hungary, born by 1162 in Hungary.**
1174, Helean married to Leopold V of Austria.

***
94555180. King Bela III of Hungary
~1150, Bela born in Hungary, s/o 189110360. King
   Geza II of Hungary & 189110361. Euphrosyne of
   Kiev.
[Undated] Bela educated in in the court of the
   Emperor of Constantinople.

[--Duke Bela--]
By 1162, King Géza organized a separate appanage
   duchy, containing Dalmatia, Croatia and other
   territories, for his younger son, Béla.
5/31/1162, Bella's father died, his brother Stephen III
   succeeding.

[--Bela & Maria--]
1163, Bela 1st married to Maria Comnena, d/o
   Emperor Manuel I Comnenus.
1169, Bela and Maria separated.

[--King Bela--]
1172, Bela succeeded his brother Stephen III of
   Hungary.
Aft. 9/24/1180, King Bela III of Hungary invaded and
   captured Croatia, Dalmatia and the Srem from the
   Byzantine empire.
1182, King Bela had his 1st son Emerick crowned to
   insure succession.
1184, King Bela III took Beograd, Branicevo and the
   valley of the Morava river from the Byzantine
   empire.
1185, Emperor Isaac (189118302) and King Bela III
   made a peace agreement, which included Isaac
   marrying a daughter of King Bela.

[--Bela & Margaret--]
1186, Bella married Margaret Capet, widow of Henry
   'the young king' of England, d/o 189110370. King
   Louis VII Capet.

1188, King Bela gave his youngest son Andrew the principality of Halych; which had rebelled against their ruler Prince Vladimir II Yaroslavich. [King Bela had imprisoned Vladimir.]

1/21/1190, Isaac II Angelus concluded the Treaty of Anrianople [negotiated with the help of King Bela III] with Emperor Frederick I, agreeing to provide transport for his forces from Hellespont to Asia Minor.

1190, Isaac, with the help of King Bela III, invaded and defeated the Serbian Grand Prince Stefan Nemanja [of Rascia] in battle. By Treaty, Serbia remained independent, but was under Byzantine influence.

10/1191, Emperor Isaac met with his father-in-law King Bela III.

4/23/1196, Bela died, leaving a large amount of money to fulfill his crusader's oath.

Children of Bela and ?:
❖ **Emerick of Hungary, born by 1182 in Hungary.**

1182, King Bela had his 1st son Emerick crowned to insure succession.

12/1197, Andrew II. Emerick's younger brother, with the help of Leopold V, duke of Austria, defeated his brother in battle near Macsek. Andrew forced his brother Emerick to grant him the duchies of Croatia and Dalmatia. (S) Pope Innocent III, Moore, 2003, P73.

1199, King Emerick defeated his brother Andrew in battle; Andrew escaped to Austria. Through papal mediation, Andrew and Emerick made peace and Andrew was restored to Croatia and Dalmatia.

1200, Emerick and Andrew were again at war. Andrew was imprisoned in Croatia. Andrew escaped again.

Aft. 8/26/1204, King Emerick, in ill health, named Andrew to govern the kingdom during his son's minority.

1204-05, King Emerick died.

5/7/1205. Emerick's son Ladislaus III died, his uncle Andrew succeeding.

❖ **Margaret of Hungary, born ? in Hungary.**

1/1186, Emperor Isaac II Angelus married 2nd Margaret of Hungary, d/o King Bela III, receiving the valley of the Morava river as her dowry. (S) The Wars of the Balkan Peninsula, Madrearu, 2008, P71.

❖ **Andrew II of Hungary (47277590), born ~1177 in Hungary.**

***

47277590. King Andrew II of Hungary &
   47277591. Queen Yolande de Courtenay &
   94555256. Queen Gertrude of Meran

~1177, Andrew born in Hungary, 2nd s/o 94555180.
   King Bela III of Hungary.

~1185, Gertrude born in Merania, d/o §§Duke
   Berthold IV of Merania (b.~1159, d.1204) &
   Duchess Agnes of Rochlitz (b.~1165,
   d.3/25/1195). [Meriania near the top of the
   Adriatic sea, SW of Hungary, then a part of the
   Holy Roman Empire.]

1182, King Bela had his 1st son Emerick crowned to
   insure succession.

1188, King Bela gave Andrew the principality of
   Halych; which had rebelled against their ruler
   Prince Vladimir II Yaroslavich. [King Bela had
   imprisoned Vladimir.]

1189, Duke Berthold a standard bearer in the 3rd
   crusade.

[--Prince Andrew--]

1189, Prince Andrew's forces suppressed a rebellion of
   boars in Halych. Soon after, Vladimir escaped
   prison and took back control of Halych.

3/25/1195, Gertrude's mother died.

4/23/1196, Andrew's father Bela died leaving a large
   amount of money to fulfill his crusader's oath.

[--Duke Andrew--]

12/1197, Andrew, with the help of Leopold V, duke of
   Austria, defeated his brother in battle near Macsek.
   Andrew forced his brother Emeric to grant him the
   duchies of Croatia and Dalmatia. (S) Pope Innocent
   III, Moore, 2003, P73.

1198, Pope Innocent III asked duke Andrew to fulfill
   his crusade promises in the Holy Land. [Instead,
   Andrew attacked Zahumlje and Rama.] (S) Pope
   Innocent III, Moore, 2003, P31.

1198, Andrew succeeded in having Croatia, Dalmatia
and other smaller territories declared semi-
independent, creating a new power center in
Hungary. (S) A History of Hungary, Sugar, 1994,
P23.

~1198, Yolande born in France, d/o 94555182. Peter
II de Courtenay & 94555183. Yolanda of Flanders.

1199, King Emeric defeated Andrew in battle; Andrew
escaped to Austria. Through papal mediation,
Andrew and Emeric made peace and Andrew was
restored to Croatia and Dalmatia.

[--Andrew & Gertrude--]

~1200, Andrew married Gertrude.

1200, Brothers Emeric and Andrew were again at war.
Andrew was imprisoned in Croatia. Andrew escaped
again.

Aft. 1200, The Andechs along the Croatian and
Hungarian border built a strong alliance with
Andrew. (S) Southeastern Europe in the Middle
Ages, Curta, 2006, P399.

8/12/1204, Gertrude's father died, buried at Andechs
monastery, DieBen, Bavaria.

Aft. 8/26/1204, King Emeric, in ill health, named his
brother Andrew to govern the kingdom during his
son's minority.

10/1204, Andrew's brother died leaving a son Ladislas
born in 1199. Emeric's wife Constance of Aragon
escaped with her son to Austria.

5/7/1205, Andrew's nephew Ladislas died in Austria.

[--King Andrew--]

5/29/1205, Andrew crowned King of Hungary.

1205, Andrew attacked his neighbors and became
King of Galicia (Poland) and Lodomeria.

1208, Andrew invaded Halych.

1209, King Andrew II confirmed by a Golden Bull all
the freedoms and estates that had been acquired
by the Knights Templars.

1210, King Andrew invited the Teutonic Knights, led by Grand Master Herman Salza to wage war against the Cumans, a nomadic Turkish tribe. (S) Ecclesiastical Review, V56, 1917, P39.

1211, Andrew gave Burzenland in Siebenbürgen [Transylvania] in the south to the Teutonic Knights to be a buffer against the Kumans. (S) History Teacher's Magazine, V9, 1918, P365.

1212, Andrew again invaded Halych.

1213, King Andrew put his son Coloman on the Galician throne and tried to replace Orthodox bishops with his own Latin priests. (S) Prince, Saint, and Apostle, Korpela, 2001, P160.

9/24/1213, Queen Gertrude murdered by nobles who resented privileges accorded to her German barons and her lavish spending. [Only the leader of the conspirators was executed.] (S) Women and Gender in Medieval Europe, Schaus, 2006, P236.

[--Andrew--]

1214, Andrew began to finance his crusade by selling and mortgaging property and debasing his coinage.

1214, Andrew and Leszek, duke of Poland, divided Halych between Hungary, and Poland. [Andrew did not live up to his end of the agreement and he was eventually driven from Halych. By another agreement part of Halych was given to his son Coloman.]

[--Andrew & Yolande--]

2/1215, Andrew married Yolanda [niece of Henry I, Emperor of Constantinople, who arranged the marriage]. (S) The Late Medieval Balkans, Fine, 1994, P101.

4/1215, Pope Innocent III proclaimed the 5th crusade in a papal bull. King Andrew was excused from immediate participation by the Pope because of civil war in Hungary. (S) A History of the Crusades, Runciman, 1987, P146.

7/11/1216, Yolanda's uncle died, and Andrew attempted [unsuccessfully] to have himself crowned Emperor of Constantinople.

7/16/1216, Pope Honorious III succeeded Pope Innocent III.

1217, Andrew issued multiple charters witnessed by Master Garin of Montaigu. (S) Central Convent of Hospitaller and Templars, Burgtorf, 2008, P521.

8/23/1217, King Andrew arrived at Spalato with 10,000 horsemen and a "host" of crusaders. Andrew had arranged with Venetians to transport his forces; but they did not have enough ships for the size of the army. [Duke Leopold VI of Austria was also on crusade, traveling by a different route with multiple brothers-in-law of King Andrew.]

9/1217, After a delay to get more ships, King Andrew embarked from Spalato on crusade. (S) The Oxford History of the Crusades, Riley-Smith, 2002, P149. [Both Clissa and Spalato were held by the Knights Templars in the name of King Andrew.]

10/9/1217, Andrew landed his forces at Cyprus; then they proceeded to Acre, where they met up with the forces of Duke Leopold of Austria.

11/10/1217, Andrew's forces defeated the forces of Al-Adil I, brother of Saladin, sultan of Egypt, at the battle of Bethsaida; but the forces retreated to fortresses of Mount Tabor which Andrew could not capture.

1/18/1218, Andrew left for his return to Hungary. Duke Leopold remained in the Holy Land.

1218, King Andrew returned via Tripoli and Antioch, stopping at Krak des Chevaliers and Margat to help the Hospitallers with construction of their facilities. On a stop in Nicaea there was an attempt on his life. Andrew returned with a large number of Jews and Muslims to whom he entrusted the collection of taxes. (S) The Biographical Dictionary, V2, Pt2, 1843, 659.

1219, King Andrew's son Bela had been sent to Armenia, and Andrew and made a request of the

Pope to commission the Hospitallers and Templars to guard his son. (S) The Hospitallers, Borchardt, 2007, P193.

1220, Andrew handed over the administration of Slavonia, Dalmatia, and Croatia to his son Bela.

1221, The recently establish Order of Dominicans sent members into Hungary. 32 of the monks were drowned in one day by the Bosnians. (S) London Quarterly Review, V4, 1855, P38.

1222, Andrew issued the "Magna Charta of Hungary" [Golden Bull] confirming privileges. Nobles and the church were to be exempted from taxes. No noble was obliged to follow the king into a foreign war. No foreigner to hold office without consent of the council of the realm. ... (S) Select Documents Illustrating Medieval and Modern History, Reich, 1905, P637. [Similarities indicate the framers of the Bull had knowledge of the Magna Carta of England. The Primate of Hungary had visited Stephen Langton, who drafted the Magna Carta, at Canterbury in 1220.]

6/6/1224, Andrew made a peace agreement with Leopold, duke of Austria.

1224, The Teutonic Knights established in Siebenbürgen sent a petition to Pope Honorius III asking to be placed under direct papal authority. [Independence from King Andrew.] (S) Oath of Fealty, Scott, 2009, P105.

1224, King Andrew issued the "Andreaneum", giving special rights to the Germans living on the royal land around Sibiu in Transylvania. (S) Contents and Addresses of Hungarian Archives, 2009, P65.

1225, Pope Honorius III instructed Ugrinus, archbishop of Kalocsa to warn King Andrew II of Hungary to stop giving Jews and pagans preference in appointments to public office. [Andrew likely sold these offices because he had found his country bankrupt when returning from crusade.] (S) The Apostolic See and the Jews, V7, Simonshohn, 1991, P150.

1225, Andrew issued a charter, to Master Garin of Montaigu. (S) Central Convent of Hospitaller and Templars, Burgtorf, 2008, P523.

1225, King Andrew expelled the Teutonic Knights by force from Burzenland because they were expanding their territory. (S) History Teacher's Magazine, V9, 1918, P365.

1226, King Andrew, needing money, farmed out the royal revenues to Jews. (S) The Jewish Encyclopedia, V6, 1912, P494.

1228, King Andrew granted to his chief treasurer Denys an estate near Cluj.

1230, Frederick II, duke of Austria, attacked the western borders of Andrew, defeating the Hungarians in Halych.

1231, Andrew led forces into Halych to secure his youngest son's rule.

12/1232, Pope Gregory IX admonished King Andrew II to correct the wrongs in Hungary including the oppression of Christian poor by Jews and Moslems in public office. Through Robert, archbishop of Gran, King Andrew [alone] was placed under an interdict [excommunicated.] (S) The Apostolic See and the Jews, V7, Simonshohn, 1991, P151.

8/20/1233, Andrew negotiated the rights of the clergy with a papal legate called the Agreement of Bereg.

1233, Yolanda died; buried in the abbey of Igris.

[--Andrew--]

5/14/1234, Andrew married Beatrice D'Este.

1234, Andrew excommunicated for violating the Agreement of Bereg.

1235, Andrew invaded Austria and forced Frederick II into a peace agreement.

1235, Andrew's excommunication lifted by the Pope.

5/28/1235, Andrew's daughter Elisabeth [born 1207, died 11/10/1231] canonized [for her Christian charity following the ideals of Francis of Assisi.]

9/21/1235, Andrew died, his son Bela IV succeeding.

(S) The Crusades and the Military Orders, Runciman, 2001. (S) History of the Latin Christianity, Milman, 1889.

Child of Andrew and Gertrude:
- ❖ **Bela IV (47277628), born 1206 in Hungary.**

Child of Andrew and Yolande:
- ❖ **Yolande of Hungary (23638795), born 1216 in Hungary.**

***

47277628. King Bela IV of Hungary & 47277629. Queen Maria Laskarina

1206, Bela born in Magyar [Hungary], d/o 47277590. King Andrew II of Hungary & 94555256. Queen Gertrude of Meran.

9/24/1213, Bela's mother, Queen Gertrude, murdered while King Andrew was on a campaign in Galicia.

1219-20, Maria Laskarina born in Nicea, d/o 94555258. Emperor Theodore I Lascaris of Nicaea & 94555259. Empress Marie de Courtenay.

1222, Maria's father died.

9/1222, Maria's mother died.

1222, Bela's father issued the Golden Bull, the basis for the Hungarian constitution. [Similarities indicate the framers of the Bull had knowledge of the Magna Carta of England. The Primate of Hungary visited Stephen Langton, who drafted the Magna Carta, at Canterbury in 1220.] Bela did not approve of this document.

1227, Genghis Khan died. He had arranged to divide his kingdoms, the largest going to Ogedei Khan the "Great Khan". His son Batu Khan the "Firm" of the Blue Horde launched an invasion of Russia, Hungary and Poland.

[--King Bela--]

1227, Cumans were permitted to enter Hungary and Bela took the title King of the Cumans.

1235, Two Dominican monks, Julian, and Bernard, had been in search of "ancient Hungary". Bernard died on the journey, but Julian returned with news of an approaching peril, the Mongols [aka Tatars, with an army of possibly 130,000.]

9/21/1235, Bela's father died.

[--King Bela--]

10/14/1235 in Esztergom, Bela crowned king of Hungary. Bela's initial concern was the consolidation of his nobles under his power, imprisoning several who did not support his rule. [Mikhail, prince of Chenigov, used this opportunity to occupy Galicia.] (S) Mikhail, Prince of Chernigov; Dimnik, 1981, P97.

1236, Bela supported Daniil Romanovich in his attacks on Mikhail, prince of Chenigov, in Galicia. [Daniil had fled to Hungary in 1235.]

11/1237, The Mongols besieged Ryazan [Russia] and destroyed the city.

2/7/1238, The Russian capital of Vladimir-Suzdal was captured and burnt by the Mongols. Batu Khan divided his armies and began ransacking Russian cities.

1238, Bela granted privileges to the city of Trnava.

[--Bela & Maria--]

By 1238, Bela married Maria.

3/2/1239, Bela authorized more Kumans, fleeing from the Mongols, to enter Hungary, led by a chief named Koten. Kotony asked to settle in Hungary, where he would help defend against a common foe. Bela assented.

1239, Koten, chief of the Kuman, baptized.

By 1240, Batu Khan sent more than five messengers to Bela who never returned. Batu was demanding the return of the Cumans and threatening Bela.

1240, Knowing that the Mongols were getting close, Bela solicited aid from the Pope, the Germans, and other neighboring monarchs. Only Frederick, duke of Austria, pledged support. Defensively, Bela blockaded the Carpathian passes and sent forces to his eastern frontier. To impress on his people the danger, Bela ordered blood-stained swords to be carried by his messengers. The Mongols easily defeated Bela's eastern forces, and also sent an army into Poland, and up the Danube, to cut off support for Hungary from western Europe.

12/6/1240, The Mongols captured Kiev, Russia.

1241, Bela sent Maria and their son to the fortress of Hainburg [in present day Bratislava, 20 mi. east of

ViennaSlavonia.] Bela crossed the Danube and encamped near Pest.

1241, Koten, chief of the Kuman, assassinated after a captured Mongol turned out to be a Cuman. [The Cumans were a very large people covering a vast expanse in Russia.] Many Cumans then fled towards the lower Danube to Bulgaria.

4/1241, Bela, with a force of 50-60 thousand, surprised Batu with an attack. Bela's mounted and armored knights were superior in small-engagement tactics. Batu retreated to more advantageous ground. [Where he stopped, Batu had the advantage of high ground for his encampment, with Bela encamped on an open plain. They attacked at night, surrounding the forces of Bela.]

4/11/1241, Bela defeated by the Mongols at the battle of Mohi in Austria. They had the help of Duke Frederick, who was ceded the counties of Monson, Sopron and Vas. Bela's younger brother Coloman died from wounds sustained in the battle. Bela and his family fled to Trau, Dalmatia, pursued by Mongols under command of Khadan.

5/1241, Bela again appealed unsuccessfully to Pope Gregory IX and Emperor Frederick II.

12/1241, The Mongols received news of the death of their Great Khan Ogotaj.

2/1242, Crossing the Danube, the Mongols were unsuccessful in their attacks on fortified cities in Germany. A month later Batu left Hungary, abandoning his plans to invade Germany. [Batu eventually settled on the Volga in Russia and died 1256.]

5/1242, Bela returned to Hungary, which had been devastated. Bela arranged for food from other countries, reconstruction of towns with walls, and the building of castles – which the Mongols were unsuccessful in capturing. Bela encourage immigration, and many were returning Kumans.

6/7/1243, Bela granted privileges to the Spis Lancers.

1244, Bela attacked Bosnia.

[--Kings Bela and Stephen--]

1245, Bela's son Stephen crowned as a Junior King, given Croatia, Slavonia, and Dalmatia.

1246, Bela concluded a peace agreement with duke Danilo of Galicia.

1246, Bela reclaimed the counties he had given up to the Duke of Austria in 1241.

6/15/1246, Bela's forces repelled those of attacking Duke Frederick of Babenberg (Austria) at the Leitha river, killing Frederick, and ending his line of succession. Bela had a claim to the inheritance.

1247, Bela gave the Knights of St. John the southeastern borderlands in exchange for their supplying armored calvary and the building of defensive fortresses.

9/2/1248, Bela granted a charter of privileges on Nitra.

1248, Bela issued a document stating, "it is the power of the king that demands that he increase, not minimize his grants."

4/13/1249, Bela granted property and privileges to persons from Sena.

1250, Bela elevated royal soldiers, free owners of small estates willing to serve under the king's command, to nobility.

1250, Bela attacked Styria, formerly controlled by Frederick of Babenberg.

6/15/1251, Bela established the Premonstratensian monastery in Klastor pod Znievom.

1253, Bela attacked Bosnia on succession of Ottokar II. Ottokar agreed to let Bela control Styria. (S) Rise of the Medieval World, Schulman, 2002, P331.

1254, Bela and Ottokar II, after 4 years of war, divided the disputed provinces; Bela receiving Styria. (S) A Short History of Austria-Hungary, Steed, 1914, P4.

1257, Bela ceded son Stephen the government of Transylvania when Stephen threatened war.

6/12/1257, Bela restored privileges on serfs of Liptov and Turiec who had fled from excessive burdens.

[--Duke Stephen--]
1258, Bela appointed son Stephen as Duke of Styria.

7/1260, Ottokar, offered the throne of Styria by its subjects who did not like the rule of Stephen, defeated the defending Hungarian forces.

1261, Son Stephen joined with Bela in unsuccessfully attacking Bulgaria.

3/1261, Bela recognized Ottokar as duke of Styria.

[--Bela vs. Stephen--]
1262 in Pozsony, By agreement with Bela, son Stephen took control of the kingdom east of the Danube.

1264, At war with his son Stephen, Bela captured Stephen's wife and son; and pushed Stephen into Transylvania.

3/1265, Stephen defeated Bela's army at the battle of Isaszeg.

1265, Bela reconfirmed noble privileges, returned noble's lands used as forts, and created county courts with enforcement powers. Each count was obliged to send deputies to a royal legislative assembly.

[--Bela and Stephen--]
3/23/1266, Stephen and Bela reconfirmed the 1262 peace agreement in the convent of the Blessed Virgin on Rabbit's Island.

1267, Stephen and Bela held a assembly of nobles and prelates of the Kingdom of Hungary at Esztergom.

5/3/1270, Bela died, son Stephan succeeding; buried at the Franciscan friary of Esztergom.

(S) Slovak History, Bartl, 2002. (S) The Realm of St. Stephen, Engel, 2005. (S) A History of Hungary in Biographical Sketches, Lukinich, 1937, P59. (S) The Man of Many Devices, Sebok, 1999. (S) A History of Hungary, Sugar, 1994.

Child of Bela and Maria:

❖ **King Stephen V of Hungary (23638814), born 10/18/1239 in Hungary.**

***

23638814. King Stephen V of Hungary &
23638815. Regent Elizabeth the Cuman

1238, A "monstrous and inhuman race of men" [Tartars], with a leader called Khan, was overrunning far eastern Europe.

10/18/1239, Stephen born in Buda, Hungary, s/o 47277628. King Bela IV of Hungary & 47277629. Queen Maria Laskarina.

~1239, Elizabeth born in Hungary, d/o 47277630. Chief Koten of the Cuman. [Their tribe arrived in Hungary in 1238.]

1241, Elizabeth's father assassinated. [Elizabeth's name likely came after her father converted to Christianity in 1239.]

4/11/1241, Stephen and his family fled to Trau, Dalmatia, after his father's troops were defeated by the Mongols at the Battle of Mohi.

Summer/1242, The Tatars withdrew from Hungary on news of the death of their Great Khan Ogotaj. [Modern evidence also indicates that a severe winter had diminished the Tartars ability to sustain warfare.]

[--King Stephen--]

1245, Stephen crowned as a Junior King, given Croatia, Slavonia, and Dalmatia.

1246, A royal charter identifies Stephen as King, and Duke of Salvonia. [Royal governors administered his lands.]

[--Stephen & Elizabeth--]

By 1254, Stephen married Elizabeth.

1257, Stephen's father ceded him the government of Transylvania when Stephen threatened war.

1258, Stephen appointed Duke of Styria.

1259, Stephen attacked Carinthia in retaliation of Duke Ulrich III of Carinthia's support of the Styrian rebels.

6/25/1260, Stephen crossed the river Morava to invade Ottokar's realm.

7/12/1260, Stephen defeated at the battle of Kroissenbrunn. [His father's supporting forces arrived late.]

1260, Stephen returned to Transylvania.

3/31/1261, The Duchy of Styria was ceded to the King of Bohemia at the Peace of Pressburg.

1261, Stephen joined with his father in attacking Bulgaria. [Most of the Cuman tribe had moved to Bulgaria after the assassination of Chief Koten.] Stephen's father returned to Hungary after seizing Vidin. Stephen laid siege to Lom on the Danube, and advanced as far as Tirnovo in pursuit of Tsar Constantine Tikh of Bulgaria. The Tsar avoided direct confrontation, and Stephen withdrew his troops from Bulgaria by the end of the year.

11/25/1261, Stephen holding the lands east of the Danube.

1262 in Pozsony, By agreement with his father, Stephen took control of the kingdom east of the Danube.

[--Stephen vs. Bela IV--]

1264, Stephen at war with his father seized his mother's and sister's estates. Stephen's father captured Stephen's wife and son.

Aft. 8/1/1264, Stephen's father's army, under the command of his sister Anna, crossed the Danube. Stephen retreated to the castle of Faketehalom. Anna besieged and captured Sárospatak, and seized Stephen's wife and children.

3/1265, Stephen defeated his father's army at the battle of Isaszeg.

[--King Stephen vs. Bela IV--]

3/23/1266, Stephen and his father reconfirmed the 1262 peace agreement in the convent of the Blessed Virgin on Marguerite Island.

6/1266, Stephen invaded Bulgaria, seized Vidin, Pleven, and other forts, and routed the Bulgarians in five battles. Stephen began to use 'King of Bulgaria' in his charters.

1267, Stephen and his father held a assembly of nobles and prelates of the Kingdom of Hungary at Esztergom.

1267, A double marriage alliance between King Stephen and King Charles I of Sicily. Stephen's son, Ladislaus was to marry Charles's daughter, Elisabeth; and Charles's namesake son (11819406) to marry Stephen's daughter, Maria.

[--King of Bulgaria--]

1268, Stephen successfully attacked Bulgaria, becoming King of Bulgaria. (S) Encyclopedia Britannica.

1269, Stephen made an alliance with Charles I of Anjou [the future king of Sicily.]

[--King of Hungary--]

5/3/1270, On his father's death, Stephen became King of Hungary.

5/17/1270, Stephen crowned king.

8/1270, King Stephen allied with Prince Boleslaw V of Poland against the king of Bohemia.[Stephen was in Cracow at the invitation of his sister Anna to join an alliance against Ottokar.]

9/1270, While visiting Miholjance, Stephen was gifted with the "Holy War Sword of the Scythians."

10/16/1270, Stephen concluded a peace agreement with Ottokar II of Bohemia.

12/1270, Stephen made a raid into Austria.

1/1271, Stephen and his court witnessed a miracle attributed to his deceased sister Margaret, a Dominican nun of Rabbit Island. Stephen sent an envoy to Pope Gregory seeking sainthood for Margaret. (S) Holy Rulers and Blessed Princesses, Klaniczay, 2002, P224.

5/1271, Ottokar of Bohemia invaded Hungary.

7/2/1271, Stephen had to relinquish claims to Styria, Carinthia, Carniola, and the Windish March.

8/25/1271, Stephen granted privileges on the Spis Saxons, exempting them from the jurisdiction of Spis county.

8/6/1272, Stephen died on Csepel Island, Hungary, while raising an army to rescue his kidnapped son Ladislaus; buried next to his sister in the Dominican convent on Marguerite Island.

[--Elizabeth--]

1272, Elizabeth became regent while her son was a minor.

1273-74, A nobles' revolt occurred against Queen Elizabeth Cuman, capturing and imprisoning Elizabeth.

9/1274, Supporters freed Queen Elizabeth from prison.

5/1277, Elizabeth's son declared of age to take over the rule of the kingdom.

Elizabeth died.

(S) Slovak History, Bartl, 2002. (S) The Realm of St. Stephen, Engel, 2005.

Children of Stephen and Elizabeth:

❖ **Elisabeth of Hungary, born 1255 in Hungary.**
Elisabeth married King Stefan Uros II Milutin of Serbia.

❖ **Catherine of Hungary, born ~1257 in Hungary.**
Catherine married King Stefan Dragutin of Serbia.

❖ **Maria of Hungary (11819407), born 1258 in Hungary.**

❖ **Anna of Hungary, born ~1259 in Hungary.**

5/3/1270, On the death of her father, Anna seized the
royal treasury any fled to Bohemia.

Anna married Emperor Andronikos II Palaiologos.

❖ **Ladislaus IV of Hungary, born 8/5/1262 in
Hungary.**

8/26/1278, Ladislaus a victorius commander in the
battle of Marchfeld over Ottokar II.

7/10/1290, Ladislaus assassinated.

EMPERORS

***

3025764668. Holy Roman Emperor Henry III Hohenstaufen& 3025764669. Empress Agnes of Poitou

10/28/1017, Henry born in Germany, s/o §§Holy Roman Emperor Conrad II of Worms (d.1039) & Empress Gisela of Swabia (d.1043).

9/4/1024 at Kamba, Henry's father elected King of Germany.

[--Duke Henry--]

1026, Henry made Duke of Bavaria by his father. [Not officially recognized until 7/24/1027.]

2/1027, Henry's father elected Holy Roman Emperor, and designated Henry as his heir.

4/10/27, Henry in Rome for his father's coronation.

2/1028, Henry made Duke of Swabia. [The charter identified Henry as the only son.]

[--Co-King Henry--]

4/1028, At the initiative of his father, Henry crowned co-ruler of Germany at Aachen.

[--Agnes--]

~1028, Agnes born in Poitou, d/o 6051529338. William V of Aquitaine & 6051529339. Agnes of Burgundy.

4/6/1029, Bishop Gilbert of Freising replaced deceased Bishop Bruno of Augsburg as Henry's tutor.

1031, Henry left in Bavaria by his father negotiated and signed a peace treaty with King Stephen I in Hungary.

7/1033, Henry knighted, no longer needing a tutor.

[--Henry & Gunhilda--]

5/18/1035, Henry's marriage to Gunhilda of Denmark arranged.

1038, Henry called to Italy in support of his father. On the return trip, Gunhilda died of an illness.

[--King Henry of Burgundy--]

1038, Henry made King of Burgundy.

6/4/1039, Henry's father died. Henry went on a tour of his domains.

8/13/1-39, Henry's forces ambushed in the Bohemian forest, suffering heavy losses at the Battle of Brudek.

8/15/1040, Henry conducted a successful campaign into Bohemia.

12/1041, Henry spent Christmas at Strasbourg.

9/1042, Henry began negotiations to wed Agnes.

1043, Henry's mother died.

10/1043, Henry initiated a "Day of Pardon."

[--Henry & Agnes--]

1043, Henry married Agnes.

7/6/1044, Henry successfully invaded Hungary.

1045, Henry wintered at Speyer while planning an expedition to Lorraine against Godfrey of Upper Lorraine, which was successful.

1046, Henry ended a schism with Pope Clement II.

12/20/1046, Henry held court at Sutri [near Rome.]

[--Holy Roman Emperor Henry--]

12/25/1046, Henry and Agnes crowned Emperor and Empress at Rome.

5/1047, Henry was in Verona, Italy, after which he returned to Germany.

1047-48, Henry had to deal with insurrections in Germany.

1049, King Edward of England (the Confessor) sent a fleet in support of Henry III, against the Count of Flanders.

1051-52, Henry suffered defeats in Hungary.

[--Son as King Henry IV of Germany--]

7/17/1054, Henry III had his very young son Henry IV crowned King of Germany. [Not unusual for the time.]

10/5/1056, Henry died of an illness at Bodfeld; Agnes becoming Regent to her son.

[--Empress Agnes--]

12/1056, Agnes, in forging alliances, gave away the Duchy of Carinthia.

1057, Empress Agnes, as regent for her son, took full control on the departure of Pope Victor II, who had come when Henry IV became seriously ill.

1057, Regent Agnes enfeoffed Rudolf of Rheinfelden with Swabia, appointed him administrator of Burgundy, and offered him the hand of her daughter Matilda.

1057, Pope Victor II died. His successor Stephen IX sent Hildebrand of Sovana and Anselm of Lucca (respectively, the future Popes Gregory VII and Alexander II) to Germany to obtain recognition from dowager empress Agnes in her role as regent.

1060, Agnes, acting for Henry, sent troops to Hungary in support of Andrew I. [Andrew I was defeated and fled to Germany.]

1061, Regent Agnes ceded the Duchy of Bavaria to Count Otto of Nordheim.

9/30/1061, Empress Agnes refused to acknowledge the new pope, Alexander II. He had been elected solely by the cardinals.

4/1062, The Archbishop of Cologne kidnapped 11-year-old Henry IV and became the Regent.

[--King Henry IV--]
1065, Henry IV came of age to make policy decisions.
1065, Agnes documented as being in Rome.
5/1065, Agnes returned to her homeland of Poitou.
[She would make trips back on various occasions.]
12/14/1077, Agnes died in Rome, buried at St. Peter's
Basilica.

Child of Henry and Agnes:
❖ **Henry IV Hohenstaufen (1512882334), born
11/11/1050 in Gostar, Saxony.**

***

1512882334. Holy Roman Emperor Henry IV Hohenstaufen & 1512882335. Empress Bertha of Savoy

11/11/1050, Henry born in Gostar, Saxony, s/o 3025764668. Holy Roman Emperor Henry III & 3025764669. Empress Agnes of Poitou.

9/21/1051, Bertha born in Savoy [NW Italy], d/o §§Count Otto of Savoy (b.~1015, m.1046, d.1060) & Margravine Adelaide of Turin.

[-- King Henry--]

7/17/1054, Three-year-old Henry IV crowned King of Germany.

[--Henry & Bertha--]

12/25/1055 in Zurich, Henry betrothed to Bertha.

10/5/1056, Henry's father died; Henry's wardship given to his mother, who acted as Regent. Henry became King of Italy and Burgundy on the death of his father.

1057, Empress Agnes took full control of her son on the departure of Pope Victor II, who had come when Henry IV became seriously ill.

1060, Agnes, acting for Henry, sent troops to Hungary in support of Andrew I. [Andrew was defeated and fled to Germany.]

4/1062, The Archbishop of Cologne kidnapped King Henry IV and became the Regent.

[-- King Henry--]

1065, Henry came of age to make policy decisions.

5/1065, Henry's mother Agnes returned to her homeland of Poitou. [She would make trips back on various occasions.]

[--Henry & Bertha--]

7/13/1066, Henry married Bertha of Savoy.

1069, Henry suppressed a riot in Saxony. Henry's policy of appointing commoners to high offices was not well received.

1069, Henry attempted to repudiate Bertha, who retired to Lorsch Abbey. Eventually they reconciled, the first child, a daughter, born the next year.

1071, Henry suppressed the rebellion of Otto of Nordheim, who he imprisoned [Otto released 5/1072].

1073, Many of Henry's advisors excommunicated by Pope Alexander II, who believed they were giving him bad advice.

6/9/1074, Henry captured Homburg castle in Saxony.

10/1075, Henry forced the rebelling nobility into submission.

12/25/1075 at Goslar, Henry IV recognized his infant son Conrad as his successor.

1075, Pope Gregory published 'Dictatus Papae', which had 27 axioms about papal supremacy, including the infallibility of the pope. This started a long dispute with Henry IV.

1/24/1076, Pope Gregory VII excommunicated Henry for selling ecclesiastical offices.

1076, Henry with Bertha and son Conrad travelled to Rome to meet with Pope Gregory VII. Along the way Bertha's mother joined them.

1/25/1077 in Rome, Henry absolved after doing a three-day penance.

3/14/1077, Some of the unhappy leaders elected Rudolf of Rheinfelden, Duke of Swabia, as an anti-King to Henry. [Soon after, Bishops loyal to Henry elected an anti-Pope, Clement III.]

12/14/1077, Henry's mother died.

4/1079, Frederick von Buren (756473200) created Duke of Swabia by Henrich IV, King of Germany; and betrothed to Henry's daughter Agnes.

10/15/1080, Duke Rudolf mortally wounded in battle against Henry's forces at the Battle of Elster.

[--Emperor Henry--]
1084, Henry laid siege to Rome.

4/1/1084, Henry crowned as Holy Roman Emperor in Rome by Anti-Pope Clement III.

12/27/1087, Bertha died in Mainz, buried in the Salian crypt at Speyer Cathedral.

[--Henry & Eupraxia --]
1089, Henry married 2nd Eupraxia of Kiev.

1089, Henry invaded Tuscany, a stronghold of Italian resistance.

1094, Henry separated from Eupraxia.

3/1095, At a council in Italy, Henry's son Conrad, in rebellion in Italy, confirmed Eupraxia's claim that Henry was a member of the heretical Nicolaitan sect of the church.

[--Henry--]
11/1095, Pope Urban II called for the 1st crusade.

1096, Henry gave orders to protect Jewish communities in his domain which came under attack by crusaders traveling through his territory.

5/1098, The German nobility deposed Henry's son Conrad, but elected his 12-year-old son Henry V as co-ruler, who pledged to submit to his father's authority.

9/8/1100, Antipope Clement III died.

5/1101, Henry suppressed a rebellion at Limburg.

10/1102, Henry rescued Cambrai from a Franconian siege.

1103, Henry proclaimed peace in Germany.

[--Henry abdicated--]
12/31/1105, Henry forced to abdicate by his younger son Henry V.

8/7/1106, Henry died of an illness at Leige in the Lower Lorraine, buried in Speyer cathedral [still under excommunication].

Children of Henry and Bertha:

- ❖ **Conrad born 2/12/1074 at Hersfeld Abbey in Germany.**

12/25/1075, Henry IV recognized Conrad as his successor.

1079, Conrad first named in a royal charter.

5/30/1087 at Aachen, Conrad crowned King of Germany.

1092, Conrad led a campaign in the march of Turin to establish imperial control.

7/1093, Conrad, in rebelled against his father, crowned King in Milan.

1094, Conrad reached the height of his power in Italy.

5/1098, The German nobility deposed Conrad, and elected his brother Henry V as co-ruler.

7/27/1101, Conrad died of a fever [possibly poisoned] in Florence, buried in Santa Reparata.

- ❖ **Agnes Hohenstaufen (756441167), born 1072-73 in France.**

1086, Agnes married Duke Frederick of Swabia, the first ruler of the Hohenstaufen dynasty. [11 children.]

1105, Frederick died.

Agnes married 2nd Leopold III, Margrave of Austria. [Multiple children including King Conrad III of Germany.]

9/24/1143, Agnes died.

[Agnes the paternal grandmother of Emperor Frederick I Barbarosa (189118300).]

- ❖ **Henry V, born ~1086 in Germany.**

4/1101, Henry knighted [which usually occurred at age 15.]

12/31/1105, Henry forced his father to abdicate.

5/1098, The German nobility deposed Henry's son Conrad, and elected 12-year-old Henry V as co-ruler, who pledged to submit to his father's authority.

5/23/1125, Henry died, buried in Speyer Cathedral.

133

***

189118300. Emperor Frederick I Barbarosa & 189118301. Empress Beatrice of Burgundy

1125-6, Frederick "Red Beard" [Barbarosa] born in Germany; s/o 378236600. Duke Frederick II Hohenstaufen & 378236601. Judith of Bavaria.

3/7/1138, Frederick's uncle Konrad elected King of Germany on the death of Lothar. Civil war broke out between the Ghibellines [Hohenstaufen] and the Guelfs [Welfs].

[--Frederick & Adelheid--]

Frederick 1st married to Adelheid of Vohnburg [no children.]

5/1142, Frederick's uncle King Konrad III [never crowned Emperor] and Welf leader Henry the Lion reached a peace agreement.

1143, Beatrice born in Burgundy, heiress & d/o 378236602. Count Renaud III of Burgundy & 378236603. Countess Agatha of Lorraine.

1143, Rebellious Roman citizens reconstituted the Senate and formed a commune [leaving the Pope his sanctuary in the Vatican – 12/25/1145 the pope reinvested as head of the church after recognizing the republic.]

1143-47, Frederick the Red denounced as his enemy Henry of Wolfrathshausen [young Henry the Lion, whose father had died in 1139] and invaded Bavaria [Welf lands]. Frederick captured Conrad of Dachau [who he later released without a ransom demand.]

Bef. 1147, Frederick captured the town of Zurich in Swabia.

2/1147, Frederick took the cross of a crusader in Bavaria.

[--Duke Frederick--]

4/6/1147, Frederick became duke of Swabia on the death of his father, Frederick the One-Eyed.

6/1147, Frederick attended the 2nd crusade with his uncle King Konrad III.

1147, King Konrad's crusader army left from Nuremberg going southeast to Regensburg, where they boarded ships to travel down the Danube.

9/7/1147, The crusaders reached the town of Cherevach west of Constantinople. The army camped to await those trailing behind. They were surprised by a sudden storm that caused loss of life and supplies.

10/25/1147, The Germans were ambushed by Turks [probably with help from the Greeks] at Dorylaeum. Most of the foot soldiers were killed or captured.

[--Countess Beatrice--]

1/22/1148, Beatrice's father died; she became "suo jure' countess of Burgundy.

4/1148, The German crusaders left Constantinople before the French. They were carried in Turkish ships.

6/24/1148 at Acre (west of Jerusalem), at a High Court of Jerusalem, King Louis of France, Emperor Conrad III, and Baldwin, King of Jerusalem met. The Council decided that the best move to defend the holy lands would be to retake Damascus. [To protect the route from Europe.]

1148, At Damascus, due to heat, lack of water, and disagreements on plans, the siege failed after 4 days.

1148, King Conrad led the Germans in an attack on the coastal city of Ascalon which failed.

1148, The Germans returned by ship, landing at Thessaly, Greece; where King Conrad sent Duke Frederick ahead to assess the condition of empire. Frederick traveled through Bulgaria and Pannonia.

4/1149, Frederick reached Germany; where he had several of the ministers of state executed.

1150, King Conrad's eldest son Henry died, leaving as heir the younger brother Frederick, age 4.

2/15/1152 at Bamberg, Duke Frederick with his uncle Konrad at his death; given preference over Konrad's own 6-year-old son to succeed.

[--King Frederick of Germany--]

3/4/1152 at Frankfurt, Frederick elected King of Germany. The Welf faction was headed by his maternal 1st cousin Henry the Lion.

3/9/1152 at Aachen [Aix-la-Chapelle], Frederick crowned King of Germany.

3/1152, Frederick advanced on the lower Rhine and attacked the city of Utrecht.

4/1152, Frederick celebrated Easter at Cologne [the largest city of western Europe at the time].

3/23/1153, Frederick concluded the Treaty of Constance with Pope Eugene III.

5/1153, Frederick held a general assembly at Merseburg on Whitsunday. Peter, king of the Danes, attended.

7/8/1153, Pope Eugene III died; succeeded by Pope Anastasius IV.

12/1153, Frederick held court at Speyer.

10/1154, Frederick assembled an army near Augsburg; then crossed the Alps, camping near Verona [in Lombardy, west of Venice, east of Milan – the capital], which was in rebellion. [Of modern Italy, the north part belonged to Germany, the middle to Rome, and the south was Sicily – land of King William I of Norman descent.]

11/30/1154, Frederick stopped for 5 days on the plain of Roncaglia, on the Po river, near Piacenza.

12/3/1154, Pope Anastasius IV died; succeeded by Pope Hadrian IV.

12/25/1154, Frederick celebrated Christmas near Milan.

1154-55, Frederick burned the fortress of Rosate; and then destroyed 3 other fortresses around the city; then marched through Vercelli and Turin [cities west of Milan.]

1155, Frederick attacked Chieri and Asti, which was burnt [the populace had abandoned the town on his approach].

2/1155, Frederick then laid siege to Tortona [southwest of Milan]. The fortress fell in 4 days.

4/10/1155, The city of Tottona surrendered. Frederick set the city in flames. [The city of Pavia asked Frederick to come to celebrate the victory.]

[--King Frederick of Italy--]

4/17/1155 at Pavia [halfway between Tortona and Milan], Federick crowned King of Italy [they celebrated for 3 days.]

1155, Frederick proceeded through Lombardy, to Romagna and Tuscany, to Rome, where he gained entry to St. Peter's at night. [The army was encamped at Tivoli, east of Rome.]

[--Holy Roman Emperor Frederick--]

6/18/1155 in Rome at St. Peter's Basilica, Frederick crowned Holy Roman Emperor by Pope Adrian IV. The same day, Frederick had to suppress a revolt, killing over 1000 Roman citizens who believed he should have received the crown from the people, not the Pope.

6/1155, Frederick moved his army to Albano.

7/27/1155, Frederick captured Spoleto [NNE of Rome, which had failed to pay their tribute], destroying the city.

9/1155, Frederick captured Verona [halfway between Milan and Venice] with an army of 1800.

10/1155, Frederick invested Henry the Lion with the duchy of Bavaria.

[--Frederick & Beatrice--]

6/9/1156 at Wurzburg, Frederick married to Beatrice.

7/1156, Frederick held court at Nuremburg.

9/1156 at Cologne, Frederick settled a long-term dispute between Henry Jsomirgott, his paternal uncle, and Henry the Lion, over the duchy of Bavaria. [This created the duchy of Austria.]

4/1157, Frederick guaranteed the rights of Jews in matters of law and declared that none should be forcibly converted to Christianity.

1157, Frederick, by the grace of God emperor of the Romans .. to his beloved uncle Otto [bishop of Friesing – one of the primary biographers of Frederick] ... briefly compiled ... the things performed by us since our accession to the throne, ...

8/22/1157, Frederick invaded Poland, which was in rebellion – not attending diets [similar to a parliament but included heads of churches] and not sending an annual 500-mark tribute. Duke Bolesław eventually submitted to large penalties and swore to come to the diets. [Duke Bolesław a half-brother of King Władysław (378220582), who was in exile.]

9/1157 at Wurzburg, Frederick knighted by an embassy from his aunt, the Empress of Constantinople [Bertha, sister of Conrad III].

10/1157, Frederick held a diet at Besancon in Burgundy; where he received an embassy and letter from Pope Hadrian claiming indirectly that he held his empire by the grace of the Pope.

1/13/1158, Frederick held a diet at Regensburg where he delt with issues about Hungary.

6/1158, Frederick, from the city of Augsburg, invaded Italy, supported by Henry the Lion, duke of Saxony and Bavaria. Frederick crossed the Alps arriving northwest of Verona. They then traveled south to Modoena to await additional soldiers from south of the Alps.

7/4/1158, Frederick and his army moved towards Milan and crossed the Adda.

8/5/1158, Dividing his army into 7 divisions, Frederick began a siege of Milan.

9/8/1158, The Milanese and Emperor Frederick made peace; the Milanese agreeing to swear fealty, to erect a royal palace, to pay money owed amounting to 9000 marks of silver or gold, and to provide 300 hostages.

11/11/1158, Frederick held a diet for all Italian cities and nobles at Roncaglia.

2/2/1159, Frederick celebrated Candlemas in the town of Oxximiano, where many of the nobles of Italy attended the ceremony.

4/12/1159, Planning another attack on Milan, Frederick spent Easter at Modena.

4/13/1159, The Milanese had captured his fortress at Trezzo where Frederick kept a large treasure.

[--King Frederick of Poland--]

5/30/1159, King Władysław (378220582) died in Poland, succeeded Frederick. [Frederick the nephew of King Władysław.]

6/1159, Frederick dismissed most of his Italian troops at Lodi, awaiting German reinforcements crossing the Alps.

7/15/1159, Frederick laid a trap for Milanese forces and killed or captured about 750.

7/20/1159, Duke Henry [the Lion] arrived with the forces from Germany.

7/1159, Frederick besieged Crema, aligned with Milan, at the instigation of the city of Cremona. Because of atrocities committed by the city's soldiers, Frederick executed his hostages, including a nephew of the archbishop of Milan. [During this time Frederick visited Beatrice who was staying in the fortress of San Bassano.]

9/1/1159, Pope Adrian IV [Hadrian] died; Pope Alexander III and Antipope Victor IV both elected by rival factions [and who later excommunicated each other].

9/1159, The Duke of Spoleto arrived with more forces.

10/23/1159, From Crema, Frederick wrote a letter to the Bishop of Brixen about the papal schism.

1/27/1160, Crema surrendered. About 20,000 were allowed to leave the city with what they could carry before it was looted and burned to the ground.

2/5/1160 at Pavia, Frederick called a diet at which he recognized Victor IV as Pope.

7/25/1160, Frederick held a diet at Erfurt, at which he requested reinforcements to attack Milan.

5/1161, Frederick launched an attack on Milan, after 1st offering surrender terms which were rejected.

3/6/1162, Frederick captured and destroyed Milan; "of the entire city, not a fiftieth part was left standing."

5/1162, Piacenza surrendered to Frederick, which was required to destroy it walls.

5-6/1162, Frederick made agreements with the cities of Genoa and Pisa, maritime cities of the north. [Fredrick was planning a maritime invasion of Sicily.]

7/1162, Frederick crossed the Alps into Burgundy.

8/29/1162, Emperor Frederick and King Louis, their armies camped on opposite sides of the Saone river between Dole and Dijon, "missed seeing each other" at the bridge of St. Jean de Losne. [They did not want to meet as arranged because of continuing disagreement over who should be pope.] Count Henry I "the Liberal", Count of Champagne and Troyes, the primary mediator between Emperor Frederick I and King Louis VII of France. [Soon after King Louis and King Henry II of England gave their support to Pope Alexander III.]

4/16/1163, Abbess Hildegard of Bingen [mystic, writer and composer] given letters of protection by Frederick as she undertook four extended missions through Germany. (S) Norton/Grove Dictionary of Women Composers, Sadie, 1994, P217.

6/1163 at Nuremburg, Frederick received 4 papal
   legates, 2 of them Cardinals, from Pope Alexander
   III.
10/1163, Frederick again crossed the Alps into Italy.
3/1164, Frederick held a diet at Parma and announced
   his plans to march on Rome. [But resistance was
   stiffening primarily through the League of Verona:
   Genoa, Venice, Vicenza, Padua, and Verona.]
4/26/1164, Pope Victor IV died.
6/1164, Frederick unsuccessfully attacked Verona.
4/15/1165, at Rouen, Empress Matilda, d/o King
   Henry I, refuses to see ambassadors of the
   Emperor Frederick [who wanted to negotiate
   marriages of King Henry II's daughters – Matilda's
   son. King Henry II, accepted the ambassadors.]
5/23/1165 at Wurzburg, Frederick held court and
   recognized Paschal III as Pope [replacing Victor
   IV]. Because they would not support Paschal, the
   Cistercians were expelled from Germany.
12/25/1165, Frederick celebrated Christmas at
   Aachen, when he began the process of canonization
   of Charlemagne.

[--Frederick attacks the Papal states--]
10/1166, Frederick invaded Italy with Rome and the
   associated papal states as his target. [William I of
   Sicily had died the previous May, leaving a minor
   as his heir; the main papal alliance in opposition to
   Frederick.]
1167, Frederick laid siege to Ancona.
5/29/1167, Frederick's forces defeated the communal
   Roman army at the battle of Monte Porzio,
   southeast of Rome. [Frederick was still at the siege
   of Ancona.]
7/24/1167, Frederick and his army arrived at Rome.
   On the Tiber river they first took Monte Maria, then
   the castle of St. Angelo, and then set fire to the
   church of Santa Maria in Turi. Pope Alexander III
   fell back to a fortified castle near the Coliseum.

Eventually, Pope Alexander had to flee [disguised as a pilgrim.]

[--Empress Beatrice--]

8/1/1167 in St. Peters, Beatrice crowned Empress of the Holy Roman Empire by Pope Paschal. [The next day a severe storm caused the sewers to overflow. Disease then ravaged his army, and Frederick retreated to Germany.]

9/12/1167, Frederick and his army encamped at Pavia.

12/1/1167, The League of Verona combined with the League of Cremona, creating a 16-city alliance seeking independence from Frederick. [This later became known as the Lombard League.]

2/1168, By arrangement of Frederick [in 1165], King Henry II of England's eldest daughter, Matilda, married Henry the Lion, duke of Saxony [who had not accompanied Frederick on his campaign against Rome.]

[--Frederick returns to Germany--]

1168, Frederick, with only a small force, decided to return to Germany via Savoy [rather than cross the Alps where he could be attacked and have little maneuverability.] Attacked on the way, Frederick fled in disguise.

3/1168, Frederick reached Burgundy, from where he returned to Germany.

1168, Frederick built up fortresses in Dahn and Trifels; and began a 6-year program of construction within Germany.

6/24/1168 at Bamberg, Frederick named his younger son Henry as King of the Romans.

4/20/1169, Frederick celebrated Easter at Alsace.

1169, Frederick granted the city of Poppenhusen important commercial privileges. (S) Families of German Ancestry, Schlegel, 2003, P99.

1170, Frederick limited the powers of church advocates, and barred all but bishops invested with regalia to coin money.

2/1171, Emperor Frederick met King Louis VII of France at Maxey-sur-Vaise to discuss the papal issue, and outstanding issues between the Empire and France.

1172, Frederick planned another expedition into Italy.

1173, Frederick began 4 new 14-day annual fairs, 2 at Aachen and 2 at Duisburg, during which all traders were exempt from paying dues.

1174, Humbert III of Savoy, "the Saint", siding with the Pope Alexander III, was deprived of many of his titles in war against Emperor Frederick I.

[--Frederick returns to Germany--]

9/1174, Frederick crossed the Alps with an army of mercenaries, mostly from Brabant, attacking Piedmont and Susa. [Christian of Mainz was already in Lombardy with a small army sent earlier by Frederick.]

10/1174, Frederick laid siege to Alessandria [Italy].

4/13/1175, Frederick ended the siege at Alessandria with the approach of a coalition of northern Italian armies; and retreated to Pavia.

5/29/1176, Frederick defeated and wounded at the battle of Legnano near Milan by the Lombar league. Frederick had been supported by the forces of Count Floris III of Holland.

11/1176, By the Peace of Anagni, Frederick recognized Alexander III as Pope.

12/12/1176, Frederick completed a treaty with the city of Cremona. [Which was followed by agreements with many other cities.]

7/21/1177, Frederick signed peace agreements with Sicily and the Lombardy League, which is known as the Treaty of Venice.

7/24/1177, Frederick brought to San Niccolo del Lido by Venetian galleys where 3 Cardinals absolved him of excommunication.

8/1/1177, Count Floris III of Holland, a guarantor for
Emperor Frederick in an agreement with Pope
Alexander III [Treaty of Venice – considered the
crowning achievement of Frederick's reign – his
imperial majesty was now recognized by all
Christendom]. (S) Contemporary Numismatics,
Loon, 1995, P35.
12/4/1177 at Osimo, Frederick published an edict on
the administration of justice.

[--King Frederick of Burgundy--]

1178, Frederick crossed the Alps at Geneva and
proceeded into Burgundy.
7/30/1178 at Arles, Frederick crowned King of
Burgundy [his first visit to that region of
Burgundy.]
10/31/1178, Frederick arrived at Spires in Germany.
[At this time Frederick came into direct conflict with
Henry the Lion.]
1/13/1179 at Worms, Frederick was ready to arbitrate
a trial between Henry the Lion and his protesting
Saxon nobles. [Henry did not show.]
1179, Frederick bought the extensive "allods" of Count
Welf VI in Swabia and acquired the counties of
Salzbach and Pfullendorf [which he gave to a son.]
1/1180 at Wurzburg, After multiple attempts to get
Henry to appear at proposed trials; Frederick
charged him with treason and declared his fiefs
forfeit.
7/1180, Henry the Lion's town of Lubeck surrendered
to a siege of Frederick. Henry the Lion took refuge
in the fortress of Stade in northern Saxony.
8/30/1181, Pope Alexander III died; succeeded by
Lucius III.
11/1181 at Erfurt, Henry the Lion threw himself on the
mercy of Frederick, who banished him for 3 years,
and granted him the two cities of Brunswick and
Luneburg. [Henry left for England.]

1182, The city of Lubeck submitted to Frederick, who bestowed on it the title of an Imperial city. (S) History of Vandalia, V1, Nugent, 1766, P337.

1182, At a diet at Regensburg, Frederick ordered axes to be brought into the hall, threatening the attending Czech magnates with death for their behavior. (S) Ritual and Politics, Dalewski, 2008, P66.

6/25/1183 at Constance, Frederick personally signed a peace agreement with Lombardy made at Piacenza [which also ended the city of Alessandria and constituted the city of Caesarea.]

1183, Duke Hendrik III of Limburg supported the election of Fulmar as archbishop of Trier [opposed by Emperor Frederick who wanted Rudolf, provost of St. Peter, to have the position.]

5/1184, Frederick at the diet of Mainz. Frederick knighted his 2 eldest sons, Henry VI and Frederick (originally named Conrad).

10/1184, Frederick arrived at Verona to meet with Pope Lucius. Frederick was hoping to settle the disputes between the Church and the Empire, so that he could get his son Henry crowned Emperor; Lucius was looking for help to get back into Rome. [During the same time, Frederick gave Henry the Lion's estates in Milan and Liguria to Obizzo d'Este.] Neither got what they wanted; but they did agree to another crusade, and to outlaw the Catharist [Albigensian] heresy developing in the church.

11/15/1184, Beatrice died at Jouhe [now in eastern France]; buried at Speyer Cathedral, Bamberg, Germany.

[--Frederick--]

1885, Frederick spent the latter half of the year in Tuscany and central Italy.

11/25/1185, Pope Lucius died; succeeded by Urban III [who retained his title as archbishop of Milan.]

1/27/1186 in Milan, Frederick directed the wedding of his son Henry [without the Pope's consent.]

5/17/1186, Pope Urban declared Folmar the true archbishop of Treves, in violation of the Concordat of Worms; and urged Cremona to lead a revolt against Frederick [threatened by Frederick, they did not comply].

6/1186, Frederick ordered his son Henry to invade the Papal states. He quickly conquered the north half and began a siege of Orvieto.

By 11/1186, Frederick returned to Germany where he held a diet at Gelnhausen and then at Nuremburg.

7/1187, The Christian army of King Guy of Jerusalem was extinguished at the battle of the Horns of Hattin.

1187, Emperor Frederick met King Philip of France on the banks of the Meuse river between Ivois and Mouzon. They renewed their pact of alliance against King Henry of England and the Welfs of Germany.

10/2/1187, Jerusalem fell to Vizier Salah-ed-Din Yusaf ibn Ayub [Saladin].

10/24/1187, Pope Urban died; succeeded by aging Gregory VIII; who immediately sent a letter to Frederick saying it was not the business of the Pope or his Cardinals "to take up arms and give battle"; reversed excommunications of Folmar; and sent a letter to Henry VI addressing it to the "elected emperor of the Romans."

12/17/1187, Pope Gregory VIII died at Pisa; succeeded by Clement III; who invited Henry VI to escort him to Rome. [Frederick was not unchallenged in all of Germany and Italy.]

[--Frederick the Crusader--]

3/1188, Frederick took the cross of a crusader at the Diet of Mainz, aka the Diet of Christ. Count Floris III of Holland and his son William joined Frederick.

5/11/1189, 20,000 crusaders assembled at Ratisbon; formed into battalions of 500, departed.

1189, The crusaders traveled overland through Hungary, Serbia, and Bulgaria. [English and French led armies were also enroute.]

8/16/1189, Frederick's army took Trajan's pass by assault against the Greeks. [Emperor Isaac II Angelus instigated the Greek resistance to the crusader army.]

9/1189, Emperor Frederick sent an embassy to Isaac II, which Isaac took hostage. Because of this, Emperor Frederick threatened to attack Constantinople.

10/1189, Frederick's forces to captured Hadrianople.

1/21/1190, Emperor Isaac II Angelus concluded the Treaty of Anrianople with Emperor Frederick I, agreeing to provide transport for his forces from Hellespont to Asia Minor.

5/18/1190, Frederick and his army reached and captured Iconium [modern Konya, Turkey.]

6/10/1190, Frederick died, drowned in the Saleph river [Turkey] while wading his horse across; buried at the church of St. Peter, Antioch. [Many of the army turned around, but a force of about 5000 proceeded to the Holy land.] Frederick was succeeded by his son Henry VI.

(S) The Deeds of Frederick Barbarossa, Mierow, 1953. (S) Frederick Barbarossa, Pacaut, 1970.

Family notes:

The Hohenstaufens aka "Ghibellines", the Bavarians as "Guelfs" or "Welfs" – the 2 most powerful families in Germany at the time; a collection of 1600 individual principalities.

Children of Frederick and Beatrice:

❖ **Beatrix of Burgundy (39979494), born 1162 in Germany.**

Beatrix married Guillaume II de Thiern, Comte de Chalon-sur-Saône.

1179, Beatrix died in the birth of her daughter.

Daughter: Comtesse Beatrix de Chalon (19989747).

❖ **Frederick V, born 7/16/1164 in Germany.**
11/28/1170, Frederick, duke of Swabia, died.

❖ **Henry VI, born 11/1165 in Germany.**
1/27/1186 in Milan, Henry married Constance, d/o &
    heiress of William II of Sicily.
4/1191 in Rome, Henry and Constanced crowned.
12/25/1194 at Palermo, Henry crowned King of Sicily.
9/28/1197, Holy Roman Emperor Henry VI died at
    Messina of malaria [or poisoned].
Child:
  • **Holy Roman Emperor Frederick II**.

❖ **Conrad [Frederick VI], born 2/1167 in
Germany.**
1/20/1191, Frederick VI, duke of Swabia, died at Acre
    from disease.

❖ **Otto I, born 7/1170 in Germany.**
1/13/1200, Otto, count of Burgundy, killed at
    Besancon.

❖ **Conrad II, born 3/1172 in Germany.**
8/15/1196, Conrad, duke of Swabia and Rothenburg
    killed at Durlach.

❖ **Philip of Germany (94559150), born 8/1177
in Germany.**

***
94559150. King Philip of Germany & 94559151. Queen Irene Angelina

8/1177, Philip of Swabia born in Italy, youngest s/o
189118300. Emperor Frederick I & 189118301.
Countess Beatrice of Burgundy.

~1180, Irene born in Byzantium, d/o 189118302.
Emperor Isaac II Angelus & 189118303. Eirene ?.

By 1185, Irene's mother died.

~1187, As a young son, Philip entered the clergy at
Adelberg.

[--Philip in the clergy--]

4/1189, Philip made provost at the collegiate church of
Aachen Cathedral.

6/10/1190, Philip's father died on crusade; his brother
Henry succeeding.

1190-91, Philip elected Prince-bishop of Würzburg
[never consecrated].

1191, Philip accompanied his brother Henry VI, King of
Germany, and Emperor of Rome, to Italy, and gave
up his ecclesiastical vows.

[--Philip--]

1192-94, King Richard of England was held prisoner in
various German cities after being captured while
returning from the crusades. [3 trials were held
during this time, attended by Henry VI, and any of
which might have been attended by Philip.]

[--Irene--]

1193, Irene 1st married King Roger III of Sicily,
becoming Queen.

12/24/1193, Irene's husband Roger died.

1194, Philip [likely] attended his brother Henry's 2nd
Sicilian expedition; in which Irene was captured.

[--Duke Philip--]

1195, Philip named duke of Tuscany.

4/8/1195, Irene's father Isaac deposed, blinded, and imprisoned with his son Alexius; by his elder brother Alexius III.

8/15/1196, Philip became duke of Swabia on the death of his brother Conrad II at Durlach.

12/1196, Philip's nephew Frederick, age 3, elected as successor to his father who was leaving for the crusades.

3/1197, Ships with German crusaders began to leave for the Holy Land, Philip's brother King Henry one of the leaders.

[--Philip & Irene--]

5/25/1197, Philip married Irene, dowager Queen of Sicily.

1197, at Augsburg, Philip of Swabia knighted, and took the cross of a crusader. (S) Courtly Culture, Bumke, 1991, P243.

1197, Philip went to Sicily to get his nephew Frederick for his coronation [hearing of his brother's death during the trip].

9/28/1197, Philip's brother Emperor Henry died of a fever at Messina; Henry's son Frederick, age 4, succeeding. [Most of the German nobles left the crusade to return to protect their interests back home.]

1197, Philip chosen as defender of the Empire during Frederick's minority. [The kingship of a child was not popular.]

[--King Philip--]

3/8/1198, Philip elected King of Germany. He was supported mainly by the southern part of the country.

6/9/1198, Otto IV became anti-King of Germany. He was supported in the north and supported by the Pope who wanted to prevent the unification of Sicily with Germany. (S) Holy Roman Emperors.

7/12/1198 at Aachen, the coronation of Otto as King of Germany.

9/8/1198 at Mainz, Philip crowned King of Germany.

1199, Thibaut, comte de Bar, in right of his wife, bought the counties of Luxembourg, Durbuy and Laroche, with the approval of Philipp, King of Germany.

1199, King Philip of France wrote to Pope Innocent in favor of Philip as Holy Roman Emperor, and specifically against Otto IV. (S) Philip Autustus, Hutton, 1896, P166.

1199-1200, Germany essentially in a north-south civil war over who would rule.

1200, Philip and Irene gave two of Irene's diadems to the cathedral of Bamberg. (S) Catalogue of the Byzantium Coins, V1, 1999, P166.

1200, Pope Innocent issued the Deliberation, giving arguments for and against each of Frederick II, Philip of Swabia, and Otto IV as holding the title of Holy Roman Emperor. (S) Collected Works of Eric Voegelin, V20, 1997, P174.

3/1201, Pope Innocent turned his support to Otto, s/o Henry the Lion, duke of Saxony, as King of Germany.

[--Philip excommunicated--]

1201, Pope Innocent excommunicated King Philip. (S) Book of Concord, Kolb, 2000, P336.

12/25/1201 at Hagenau, Marquis Boniface of Montferrat, elected leader of the upcoming crusade, visited Philip at his Christmas court. (S) Pope Innocent III, Moore, 2003, P108. [At this time, Philip and Boniface agreed to divert the target of the crusade from Egypt to Constantinople. Philip's nephew Alexis had escaped prison and attended the court.]

10/1/1202, Philip as leader of the Ghibellines allied with the Venetians sailed on crusade from Venice against Greece with 200-plus ships [the Pope wanted them to attack Egypt; but many wanted to attack Greece for their disobedience to the Latin church.]

11/10/1202, The crusaders reached and then captured Zara.

1/1/1203, Philip sent an embassy to Pope Innocent to tell him of the capture of Zara. (S) Cambridge Medieval History, Vs1-5.

4/1203, The crusades sailed from Zara, with leader Marquis Boniface of Montferrat remaining behind.

1203, All the crusaders reached Durazzo, when Philip's young nephew Alexis was received as their emperor.

1203, Meeting resistance, the crusaders devasted the island of Corfu. About half the crusaders then separated, desiring to proceed to Syria rather than Constantinople. An agreement was reached guaranteeing later transport for the separatists to Palestine.

5/24/1203, The fleet sailed from Corfu for Constantinople. They captured the island of Andros in the process.

6/24/1203, The crusader fleet anchored off the abbey of St. Stephen, seven miles south of Constantinople. After a brief skirmish, Alexius demanded the surrender of his uncle Alexius III as a traitor and usurper.

7/5/1203, The siege of Constantinople began with a French attack on the Galata and its defensive tower.

7/17/1203, The Venetians, with a sea assault, captured 25 towers on the sea wall, and set fire to the buildings inside the walls. That night Alexius III fled to Mosynopolis.

7/1203, The Byzantine officials released imprisoned Isaac Angelus, restoring him to office.

8/1/1203, The young Alexius IV crowned co-emperor with his father Isaac Angelus. Alexius agreed to pay the crusaders and the Doge of Venice 200,000 marks to put him on the throne of Constantinople. (S) Archimedes Codex, Netz, 2007.

1203, Philip [apparently] returned to Germany at this time.

1/1204, Irene's father died.

1204, Hermann of Thuringia submitted to Philip.

[--Philip attacks Cologne--]

1/6/1205 at Aix-la-Chapelle, which is close to Cologne, Philip crowned King again by Adolf of Cologne.

5/1205, Philip, supported by the Archbishop of Cologne, began the siege of Cologne by blockading the Rhine above and below the city. Cologne was the seat of power of his rival Otto IV.

9/29/1205, Philip began a 5-day attack on Cologne, during which Otto IV was wounded.

10/1205, Failing to take Cologne, Philip captured Neuss and other castles and fortifications around Cologne before calling off the attack.

6/1206, Philip again attacked the lower Rhine.

7/27/1206, Philip defeated Otto IV at the battle of Wassenberg, west of Cologne. Otto escaped to Cologne. The Archbishop of Cologne, now supporting Otto, was taken prisoner.

11/11/1206, Philip captured Cologne.

1207, The papal ban on King Philip removed.

6/21/1208, Philip murdered at Bamberg, Germany, by Otto VIII of Wittelsbach, the Count Palatine of Bavaria, who had been promised the marriage of one of Philip's daughters. Philip had recanted and refused to support a different marriage. [The Count was killed 3/1209, his head was thrown in the Danube, and his body remained unburied for seven years.] (S) Courtly Literature, V25, 1990, P171.

[--Irene--]

8/27/1208, Irene died in childbirth at Hohenstaufen castle, in Göppingen in Baden-Württemberg, Germany.

(S) History of the Crusades, V-II, Setton, 2006. (S) Oxford Encyclopedia of Medieval Warfare, V1, 2010, P409.

Children of Philip and Irene:

- ❖ **Beatrice of Hohenstaufen, born 1198 in Swabia.**

1208, Beatrice pleaded for vengeance for her father.

1212, Beatrice married Otto IV, Holy Roman Emperor.

8/11/1212, Beatrice died without heirs.

- ❖ **Cunigunde of Hohenstaufen, born 1200 in Swabia.**

Cunigunde married King Wenceslaus I of Bohemia.

- ❖ **Marie de Hohenstaufen (47279575), born 1201 in Swabia.**

- ❖ **Elisabeth of Hohenstaufen, born 1203 in Swabia.**

Elizabeth married King Fernando III of Castile.

***

189118302. Emperor Isaac II Angelus & 189118303. Empress Eirene ?

9/1156, Issac born in Greece, s/o §§Dukas Andronikos Angelos & Duchas Euphrosyne Kastamonitissa.

~1160, Eirene born in Greece.

[--Isaac & Eirene--]

~1178, Isaac married Eirene.

9/1183, Andronikos I Komnenos [Isaac's cousin] crowned co-emperor with Alexis II [age 14] in Constantinople.

10/1183, Andronikos I Komnenos had Alexis II strangled with a bow string. [Andronikos I Komnenos was not liked.]

1184, King Bela III (94555180) of Hungary took Beograd, Branicevo and the valley of the Morava river from the Byzantine empire. [Bela likely knew Isaac since he had been educated at court in Constantinople.]

1185, Isaac's father died.

1185, While Emperor Andronikos I Komnenos was away from Constantinople, his lieutenant, Stephen Hagiochristophorites, attempted to arrest Isaac. Isaac killed the lieutenant by splitting his head with an axe and took refuge in the Hagia Sofia. (S) Byzantine Empresses, Garland, 1999, P211.

[--Emperor Isaac--]

9/1185, Isaac declared Emperor. When Andronikos I Komnenos returned, he had to flee by boat, but was captured.

9/12/1185, Isaac executed Andronikos I Komnenos.

By 1185, Eirene died [or was divorced.]

[--Isaac--]

1185, Isaac and King Bela III made a peace agreement, which included Isaac marrying a daughter of King Bela.

1185-86, Isaac increased taxes, a difficult burden for Romanian sheep farmers.

11/7/1185, Isaac defeated Norman King William II of Sicily at the battle of Demetritzes [modern Sidirokastro, Greece, on the banks of the Strymon]; but failed to take Cyprus.

1185-86, Isaac sent 80 galleys to liberate his brother Alexis III from Acre, which was unsuccessful.

[--Isaac & Margaret--]

1/1186, Isaac married 2nd Margaret of Hungary, d/o King Bela III, receiving the valley of the Morava river as her dowry. (S) The Wars of the Balkan Peninsula, Madrearu, 2008, P71.

1186, Bulgarians near Anchialos (Pomorje) attacked Isaac's fortresses in eastern Bulgaria under the leadership of Alexios Vranas.

1186, Isaac led expeditions [unsuccessful] against Bulgarians and Walachians.

1186, Isaac sent a force of 70 ships against Isaac Komnenos of Cyprus which were decimated in defeat. [Cyprus would be captured in 1191 by King Richard I of England.]

1187, Isaac made an agreement in which the Venetian Republic would provide 40–100 galleys on six months' notice in exchange for favorable trading concessions.

9/1187, Alexios Vranas, Isaac's military commander, attempted to seize Constantinople.

1/6/1188, Isaac sent an embassy to Saladin, sultan of Egypt and Syria, congratulating him on his liberation of Jerusalem. (S) The Third Crusade, Nicolle, 2005, P16.

1188, Isaac renewed a peace agreement [formerly made by Andronikos I Komnenos], with Saladin, sultan of Egypt and Syria. [Patriarch Dositheus of Constantinople offers unconditional absolution to any Greek killing a Westerner.]

6/1188, Isaac recognized the 2nd Bulgarian empire; an autonomous state with the empire granted as a lifetime possession to two Romanians, Asan, and Theodore.

1188-89, Emperor Isaac used Turkish mercenaries to ambush forces on the way to the Holy Land.

1189, Isaac and William II of Sicily made a peace agreement.

1189, King Philip Augustus of France wrote to Isaac asking permission to travel through Byzantine land on the way to the Holy Land.

9/1189, Emperor Frederick sent an embassy to Isaac, which Isaac took hostage. Because of this, Emperor Frederick threatened to attack Constantinople.

11/1189, King William II of Sicily died.

1/21/1190, Isaac II Angelus concluded the Treaty of Anrianople, negotiated with the help of King Bela III of Hungary, with Emperor Frederick I, agreeing to provide transport for his forces from Hellespont to Asia Minor.

6/10/1190, Emperor Frederick died on the way to the Holy Land. Isaac was now free to invade the Balkans.

1190, Isaac, with the help of King Bela III, invaded and defeated the Serbian Grand Prince Stefan Nemanja of Rascia in battle. By Treaty, Serbia remained independent, but was under Byzantine influence. Isaac gave Prince Stefan an imperial title.

10/1191, Emperor Isaac met with his father-in-law King Bela III.

5/1192, Isaac sent and embassy to Saladin, seeking an alliance against Western Europeans. On return, the embassy vessel was captured by Genoese ships. (S) Crusades from the Perspective of Byzantium, Laiou, 2001, P157.

11/1192, Isaac wrote to the Commune of Genoa describing the attack and asking for compensation of 96,000 hyperpyra (gold coins) and 566 nomismata (silver coins). Isaac stated that without restitution, he would take the money from Genoese merchants and those of Pisa in Constantinople.

Isaac soon received 20,000 hyperpyra from the merchants.

10/1193, Isaac wrote to the city of Genoa explaining why he had confiscated some merchandise of Genoese merchants. Genoa claimed his attackers were outlaws. Genoa and Isaac came to a settlement.

1194, Isaac defeated at the battle of Arcadiopolis (modern Lule Burgas in Turkey).

3/1195, Isaac assembled an army near the city of Cypsela for an invasion of Bulgaria.

[--Isaac blinded--]

4/8/1195, Isaac II Angelus deposed, blinded, and imprisoned with his son Alexis IV, by his brother Alexius III.

1195-6, Isaac's son Alexis IV escaped imprisonment.

4/23/1196, King Bela III of Hungary died.

12/25/1201 at Hagenau, Alexis IV visited Philip of Swabia (94559150), King of Germany at his Christmas court. [Philip married to Alexis' sister Irene.] (S) Pope Innocent III, Moore, 2003, P108.

5/1202, at Rome, Boniface of Montferrat proposed to Pope Innocent III the restoration of Isaac Angelus with the support of crusaders, which was refused. (S) Cambridge Medieval History, Vs1-5.

4/1203, Isaac's son Alexis IV joined the crusaders sailing from Zara in Greece.

[--Emperor Alexis IV--]

1203, All the crusaders reached Durazzo, where Alexis IV was received as their emperor.

6/24/1203, The crusader fleet anchored off the abbey of St. Stephen, seven miles south of Constantinople. After a brief skirmish, Alexius IV demanded the surrender of his uncle Alexius III as a traitor and usurper.

[--Co-Emperor Isaac II--]

7/1203, Constantinople was captured, and Isaac II was released from prison by the crusaders. Led by his son Alexius IV, Isaac II was restored as Emperor.

8/1/1203, The young Alexius IV crowned co-emperor with his father. Alexius agreed to pay the crusaders and the Doge of Venice 200,000 marks to put him on the throne of Constantinople. (S) Archimedes Codex, Netz, 2007.]

2/1204, Isaac died soon after his son Alexis.

(S) History of the Crusades, V-II, Setton, 2006. (S) Oxford Encyclopedia of Medieval Warfare, V1, 2010, P409.

Children of Isaac and Eirene:

❖ **Alexis IV, born ? in Byzantium.**

1203 at Durazzo, Alexis IV was received by crusaders as their emperor.

6/24/1203, Alexius IV demanded the surrender of his uncle Alexius III as a traitor and usurper.

2/8/1204, Alexis killed during a conflict between the crusaders and the people of Constantinople.

❖ **Irene Angelina (94559151), born ~1180 in Byzantium.**

Printed in Great Britain
by Amazon

26031050R00089